Mourning a
Father Lost

Mourning a Father Lost

A Kibbutz Childhood Remembered

AVRAHAM BALABAN

TRANSLATED BY YAEL LOTAN

ROWMAN & LITTLEFIELD PUBLISHERS, INC.
Lanham • Boulder • New York • Toronto • Oxford

ROWMAN & LITTLEFIELD PUBLISHERS, INC.

Published in the United States of America
by Rowman & Littlefield Publishers, Inc.
A wholly owned subsidiary of The Rowman & Littlefield Publishing Group, Inc.
4501 Forbes Boulevard, Suite 200, Lanham, Maryland 20706
www.rowmanlittlefield.com

P.O. Box 317, Oxford OX2 9RU, UK

British Library Cataloguing in Publication Information Available

Library of Congress Cataloging-in-Publication Data

Balaban, Avraham, 1944–
  [Shiv'ah. English]
  Mourning a father lost : a kibbutz childhood remembered / Avraham
Balaban ; translated by Yael Lotan.
      p.   cm.
    ISBN 0-7425-2921-5 (Cloth : alk. paper) — ISBN 0-7425-2922-3 (Paper :
alk. paper)
    I. Title.
PJ5054 .B225S5513   2004
892.4'609—dc21   2003011532

Printed in the United States of America

♾ ™ The paper used in this publication meets the minimum requirements of
American National Standard for Information Sciences—Permanence of Paper for
Printed Library Materials, ANSI/NISO Z39.48-1992.

Contents

Child of a Dream, Child of a Laboratory

I should have found some opportunity to cry. If not for the loss of a beloved father, at any rate for the loss of a father. And if not in grief, at least in anger, pity, and loss. If not for being orphaned by father's death, then for being orphaned by the death of a nonfather. And if his death was no cause for tears, his wasted life certainly was. And if not for him, I could have wept for the civilization of my childhood, whose cracking, rusting remnants lay scattered all over the place. I had been a child of a dream, of a laboratory. To this day I wake some mornings with a melody from those dreams echoing in my mind, as if I were a music box, an old dream box. If I couldn't tap into the tears at the cemetery, before the watchful eyes of the gathering, I could have wept in private, in Mom's place, or in the apartment that the kibbutz had given us for the week of mourning. I should have found some opportunity to cry, and I didn't.

My wife Raheli was waiting for me at the airport and in response to my unspoken question informed me that my father had died while I was on my way over. She looked at me sideways, cautiously, not knowing what to expect, and I did the same and observed myself from the side. I felt somewhat embarrassed, as if something improper had happened to me, or as if orphanhood conferred additional importance and attention on me as a pleasant yet shameful indulgence. I recalled my last meeting with my father, at the geriatric clinic where he lay, and his sorrow for his ending life caught me unprepared. His fear of what lay beyond his last breath touched me more deeply than I'd expected, and a shiver passed through me, close to the site which gives rise to tears. I thought about Mom and her new loneliness in the world and quickly went through all the valves that threatened to shake my body and tightened them with a firm hand. Raheli hugged me, and I watched from the sidelines as the old mechanism of suppression, camouflage, and detachment, a mechanism cultivated by the kibbutz children's homes, went into operation, like the massive, disproportionate arms of a man whose legs are paralyzed. A silent camera closely followed my facial expressions, which became stiff. I opened the trunk of the car and quietly put in my luggage. I felt my wife's hand on my arm and more than ever rejoiced in her. We hadn't seen each other for three weeks. She was supposed to visit me in Florida in a couple of weeks' time. I did not return the hug. At that moment it was all right to receive without giving. I stretched my arms and gave her a brief smile that did not reach my eyes. Since it was necessary to say something, I cleared my throat and suggested, despite my tiredness, that I drive from the airport to the kibbutz.

I

TEN OPENING DATA

Broken Skies

A.

"I'm going for a little walk," I said. Mom got up from her chair and as she came near me I was again struck by how small she'd grown in the past few years. The skin on her cheeks was dry and sprinkled with the bristles of age. Her eighty-one years had withered her arms, leaving their skin sagging and wrinkled like a deflated balloon. She kissed my arm and, red-eyed, wiped the impression of her lips from my skin. I put on my denim jacket and stepped out into the familiar midday silence of the kibbutz: the silence of flies, of rotting pecan leaves. The wintry sun exposed cracks in the house walls and in the pavement leading to the dining hall, a distance that had shrunk so much since I left the kibbutz a quarter-century ago. To the eyes that followed me from house windows and the bench in front of the dining hall I was "the son of Shprintza and Yonah who's come from America for the funeral." My fresh orphanhood lent my footsteps a strange, not unpleasant weightiness.

Beyond the dining hall my first children's house was still standing. Where our sandbox used to be there was now an old Ellis tractor, painted red. The green-trunked eucalyptuses behind the building had grown taller, dwarfing it. The first four rooms of that long structure had been my first children's house. In the next four rooms Mom looked after her kindergarten brood. I remembered the building well—the screened windows which stuck out in the back—but not the life that was lived within its walls. Only the cry, "Be a good boy, be a good boy!" still echoed among them, like the crack of a whiplash lingering after the whip has been put away. On the old laundry lines beside the house, white children's shirts shivered in the wintry wind. The wind nipped my flesh and opened a dim well of memory which soon clarified. In a moment it revealed all its forms, the forms of light and shade, of Mom's voice, of the alarm at her absence.

A wall, a white wall, blocked Mom's smell and hushed her footsteps. Now and then her voice, familiar as the taste of saliva in the mouth, spoke behind the wall or grew angry. From time to time she hung the washing on the laundry lines beside the children's house or played with her kinder- garten children on the lawn before the house. The white wall came to an end where the building ended, but it was forbidden to go to Mom even on the lawn or in the sandbox behind the house. The prohibition was imposed by strong hands lifting me brusquely in the air, surprising me on my way to Mom, even when I thought no one was looking. I am two or three years old, I believe. Now when I closed my eyes I had a sensation of feet walking on the floor of the children's house as if stepping on thick cushions. The black earth around the building is overgrown with burdock weeds. Their big leaves, rough as green sandpaper, reach my knees.

The first memory is a broken sky and darkness. I'd tried to take hold of the laundry line beside the children's house but tripped and struck my eye against the iron post with a dreadful impact. For a moment I felt that the sky had shattered like a huge glass bowl, spilling an immense light. The searing flashes were at once swallowed up by a red-and-black darkness. In my fright I covered the hurt eye with my fist. The retina retained the image of the streams of light falling and draining into the black earth. The terror of the darkness and the spilt light sharpened the pain. Mom—find Mom quickly, I thought. Mom will cool the burning eye and bring back the light. The back of Mommy's hand is dry and freckled, but the palm is warm and moist like lips. Only sink into her, only tell her what happened. Nothing existed beyond that fright, not the voice of Batya the nursemaid calling the children to lunch, not the voices of the children playing in the sandbox, only the terror of the blinded eye, only the need to reach Mom quickly. I knew with a baby's certainty that such a pain deserves Mom.

Hearing my screams Batya came running, grabbed my arm with her strong hand, and led me inside. I wanted to tell her what happened but couldn't get at the words. A cold hand pulled my hand away from the injured eye but I quickly put it back. "What happened to him?" asked a woman's voice, and Batya said, "Leave him, he'll be all right." I heard Mom's voice behind the wall and sensed that she could also hear mine.

The wall dividing the two children's houses stood firm, it returned a sharp kick for every sharp kick, a feeble kick for a weak one. It felt cold on the floor, wet and dark, scary and miserable. I held on to the covered eye and the pain to show Mom when she came, but the pain faded away and there was no point in holding on to it. Later I could open my eye. Then I went to bed, because all the children were already taking their midday nap. I lay on the bed and covered myself. I knew, with the few words available to me, that the next time I saw Mom she wouldn't be herself.

Wednesday, the second day of the shivah. Relatives and friends and kibbutz members keep coming to Mother's house. Mom sits in the chair Father used to occupy in the last years. Once he fell ill his world shrank into a triangle—its apex the table at which he sat and dozed, its other points the nearby fridge and the facing bathroom. Now Mom sits at the table and relates, again and again, to the people who have come to comfort her, what his final days were like. Even in normal times she cries easily, as though her flesh were sodden with tears, and these days her eyes are swollen from weeping. My younger sister Dinah hardly sits down. She clears empty plates from the table, serves coffee, and prepares the next meal. Since my arrival I've noticed that bereavement has restored the traditional roles, the women are responsible for getting the food, serving it, and washing up, while the men sit around the table and talk.

The mourning for my father and the sharp transition from a university town somewhere in Florida to my childhood kibbutz have honed all my senses: the voices are sharper than ever, the colors more intense, and only the sense of taste seems to have lost some of its subtlety. This hasty transition has given my memory a violent shake, crumbling the stony accretions over the far-off days, restoring their colors and sounds. Memory, the slow stalagmite of the years, dissolves into its components: water, lime, salt. My entire existence here now, morning-noon-evening, is a photograph accidentally exposed to two different views: under my warm leather shoes I feel the cold, clammy rubber boots we had to wear in winter.

B.

Gleaming whitely in my memory, a row of long stone houses—the kibbutz members' homes—stood opposite our children's home. Four rooms in each building, one per family. The rooms are as simple as a child's drawing: four walls, a door, and a facing window. No pictures or ornaments hang on the bare walls, the roofs are as flat as the sandboxes beside the children's houses. The whitewashed walls glare in the sunlight like bones in the desert. Around them are thin rows of grass which fail to cover the black soil and the deep fissures which gape in it in summer. Here and there stand ficus trees like scarecrows, a few Persian lilacs. Only the eucalyptuses have overreached the roofs. A few dozen yards east of the row of houses stand the gray concrete cubes of the communal showers and toilets (I can see the slimy whitish wooden patterns in the dusky, cool, and mysterious setting of the high-ceilinged shower room). A little to the north of the children's houses stands the dining hall, which in the evening becomes the social heart of the place. A graceless rectangular structure, but its thick walls, still bearing the decorations from the last festival, have a reassuring quality in the heavy darkness that comes down at night. Facing it is the water tower, its naked concrete bearing the marks of its original scaffolding like fingerprints. Down the hillside, beyond the dining hall, stands a row of wooden huts. The third room in the second hut is my parents' home.

Here everything is new and enthusiastic, in flight from tradition. Only the bleating of the sheep and the lowing of cows suggests a bit of grass, a possibility of roots. Everything is new and enthusiastic, yet the courtyard is as thick with rumors, rules, and regulations as that of a monastery. Everyone measures himself in the mirror of his comrades.

Here everything is new and stony, bare as the knees of a child stumbling on the hard ground. The babies are left to sleep alone in the children's house, and only the night watchman, making the rounds of the henhouses, the cowshed, and the sheepfold, peers into their room at midnight to check that nothing untoward has happened to them. On my obsessive strolls to the children's house during these days of mourning the earliest memory I've been able to dredge up is a brief scene: a chamber pot in the middle of the room and Ronni lifts a piece of turd, yellow as clay, up to his mouth. Around him three or four children stand grinning, while he laughs with pleasure—a child who knows he's being outrageously naughty. The white pajamas gleam in the dusk which is no longer night but not yet day. I see this scene from above: I must be sitting in a high-sided cot. Although there are no adults with us at the moment, I do not recall any fear. What I'm feeling chiefly is envy: they're together and I'm on my own, they've dared to slip off their beds and taste from the pot and I did not. Why, out of all the possible images from the second year of my life, did this one persist? What causes a thing to be remembered as extraordinary before life has solidified, before the ordinary has been established? Perhaps it was the astonishment and the menace. I sense that a rule is being broken, and there is a menace in its violation: so then the nurses' prohibitions can be ignored and the outcome is not punishment but delighted giggles. Or perhaps the nightly eating and drinking from the chamber pot clashed in my mind with the severe warnings that in the following years accompanied the hygienic habits instilled by the nurses, and the image remained inexplicable and disturbing.

C.

Here everything is exposed: a skeleton of a family, a skeleton of a house, a beginning of a garden. And a child whose eyes and elbows stick out like outlines for an unfinished house. We're an abbreviated family, no uncle or grandma, only Mom and Father, and they too return to their room after putting their children to bed in the children's house. When they leave, the only voice in the darkened passage is that of the nurse. The jackals know when the nurse leaves the children's house, as if her departure were an agreed signal. The first wail comes over the kibbutz's rusty fence, which passes near our children's house, rises at once to its pitch, drops for a moment, gathers strength, and tries to reach its peak again. It is joined, before it falls silent, by fresh wails from the dark field. Now they rise and fall continually, rasping the darkness. The shadows in the room move around, the scraping of their nails on the floor makes the air tremble. I breathe softly, I don't turn to the wall, to avoid exposing my back to the room beasts. They stir restlessly against the doorway. They stop beside the beds, stand and crouch, stand and crouch. I don't move my arms and legs.

Behind the children's house something is rustling in the thorns. During the day sometimes a centipede or an earwig crawls in from there and quickly hides from the nurses' yells. "Something came in, it's hiding under the bed," Nehemiah mumbles in his sleepy voice when he comes back from the toilet with Avigdora. Another child wakes. "A centipede," the whisper runs from bed to bed. Now our room is awake and soon the whole children's house. Wrapped in sheets, we cluster like penguins in the

room next to the toilets, exchanging worried looks. The single drops of
fear collect into a puddle. "They can climb on beds?" someone asks.
"They can even fly," declares another. "It's safer on the beds," says Avigdora with the gravity of a child without adults nearby. Avigdora is already
four years old.

Outside it is pitch dark. The black earth has grown hills of darkness.
Beyond lie our parents' homes. We sit on the beds in threes and fours. A
smell of sweat hangs in the air: something must be done, but what? Ronni's parents live nearest to us, the group recalls. Ronni's parents are teachers. Once—when was it?—he succeeded in calling them. Ronni sits on his
bed and starts to thump the wall with his back at regular intervals.
"Mommy," "Daddy," he calls out with every movement, dividing each
word in two equal syllables. He doesn't yell very loud, preparing for a long
campaign. His face is serious and his body sways back and forth rhythmically, as if in prayer. My tired head, longing for the warm blanket of sleep,
remembers that this happened once before—they heard and they came.
Someone peeps out of the window. Thick darkness. There's no telling if
Ronni's shouts are heading for the house or spreading through the darkness. When will the night watchman come, and how much of the night
has passed? Ronni stops for a moment, bundles himself more snugly in
the sheet, and resumes thumping the wall. The children beside him join
in the cry, "Mom-mee," "Da-dee," though these are not their Mommies
and Daddies.

D.

Mom and Father are busy building up this place, and if they can't finish
their work in time to fetch their children from the nursery or kindergarten, they ask a friend or neighbor to do this—for are we not all brothers?
The few visits by people from their hometown, generally on Passover or
the New Year, offer the nearest thing to a hug from an uncle or aunt. Mom
and Father are very busy, laboring to put flesh and sinews on the skeleton
of this settlement, and normally they only see their children for a little
while before they put them to bed. These few moments are all it takes to
remind the children of the existence of a warm body to snuggle against
and all it takes to revive the fear of abandonment. The children are sheltered by the finest theories, surrounded by nurses and educators, but the

nurses soon discover that a mother's love no more resembles her feeling for her friend's children than blood resembles sweat. The children develop survival strategies, like street kids, toughening their skin to the best of their abilities. When they grow up they will evince the selfishness of people who never got enough protection and security. The motto of the kibbutz movement—"What's mine is yours, what's yours is mine"—likewise contributed to this: in time, all that remains of it is the habit, and later the wish, that what is yours is mine. Like children who grow up too soon, they would age in time but never reach maturity. My father was in charge of the kibbutz plantations for almost forty years, and in the summer I'd go with him to the apple orchard to help him move the irrigation hoses or gather the first fallen apples. "You see," he observed to me more than once, holding out an apple with one red cheek. "The first to ripen are always the apples that were damaged by hail or pests or pecked by bird."

Remembering a Lack

Friday. We're not expecting any more visitors after lunch. My older brother, Elan, phones last instructions to his laborers, who are picking aubergines and melons. Then he takes the evening paper to Father's bed, in the central room. Mom makes her bed in the half room that has been hers since we moved into this flat some forty years ago. It was originally a room-and-a-half—the front room, in which we receive the guests, was tacked on twenty years later. "You get some rest too," Mom says, and I set out once again to walk in the direction of the dining hall and the children's houses. The day I arrived I went quite casually to look at my first children house, and since then I can't give it up. Once a day I take time out and go for extended walks through the kibbutz, in a persistent search for the place where memory is not one more snapshot in the album, but the album itself.

The central figure in this place is Mom. It's strange, considering how little we actually were together. Throughout my childhood Mom was a children's nurse and did not get home before she'd sent "her" children to their parents after supper and laid the tables for the next morning's breakfast. When she came home she would chat with Father, or rest a little, then we'd walk together to the children's house where she put me to bed. She would thus take me from a place where she was not to another place where she wouldn't be. Only on the dark dirt path between them was she wholly mine, and when she sat on the edge of my bed to sing me a lullaby. "On the shore of Kinneret Lake a splendid palace stands." Her warm soprano caressed the words, toyed with them like seawaves with an abandoned plaything. I still wake sometimes with one of her songs in my mind. Today

it seems to me that all my years at school and university were mere com-
mentaries to those lullabies. She honestly believed that she was turning a
new leaf, that she was raising children rooted in this soil and her warm
voice peeled the blanket and pajamas off my body and enveloped the bare
flesh with the honey of sweet longings. I didn't understand the words of
her songs, I only heard the yearning caress of her voice, sensed the direction of its pull and an unspoken promise: every word has a hidden shadow
in which alone can a full, true life be lived. She wanted to raise a country
boy, yet night after night she poured into me the sentiment and longings
of wide-open spaces, which she thought she'd left behind. She did so want
us to stay here, Elan and I and Dinah, who was five years younger than
me, with her and Father—as though the train of longings had a natural,
unmistakable final stop, which was this place. I would be the first to leave,
even before the end of my military service. Elan would come back for a
few years after his national service, then moved to a distant village in the
Aravah, where he still lives with his family. Dinah, like me, would not
return after the army, would finally marry and settle down in a kibbutz in
the north.

   Mom wanted to raise a Hebrew child, but the only lullabies she knew
in Hebrew were those of Kadia Molodowska—pure Warsaw wistfulness,
honey-flavored longings, a fine cookie on a gilt plate. I close my eyes and
recall the melody: "Throw open the gate—a golden coach is coming in
state: Grandpa and grandma, uncle and aunt, cousins and all are riding in
front." Even as a child, I'd close my eyes and let this melody throw open
a gate of dreams: "In Warsaw, in a quiet suburb, lives little Ruthie with
her mother." When Mom reaches the words, "Mother calls her daughter
home, the windows are ringing her name," she gets carried away and
raises her voice. This is the moment, night after night, when the words
join together behind my eyelids to form a chain of sounds which rocks me
up and down like a marvelous swing. With Father it's best to be side by
side, going the same way—to the apple orchard to shut a stopcock, or to
see the new cows from Holland. With Mom it's best to be face to face.
When she takes me up in her arms, before putting me to bed, I rock happily from side to side. Behind her back there is a tiny hole in the wall, and
into it I insert a hairpin I've taken from her hair. The mighty shock it gives
us convinces me that I should not have done it (and warned me that I'd
been told never to stick things into an electric socket, and felt that I'd

known but ignored the knowledge). But thanks to the shock I can recollect—dimly, as though the memory permeates my skin: to be held in arms,
to belong and be hugged and lack nothing, to be surrounded by firm,
warm flesh, borne upon this abundance which is my Mom.

Kadia Molodowska's golden words leave me at bedtime with an ineffa-
ble longing, an obscure promise: "Grandma and grandpa, uncle and aunt,
cousins and all riding in front . . ." The words grandma and grandpa
sound sweet, like the pastries Yehoshua's grandmother gives us when we
visit her in the cabin near the dining hall. She remains standing at the
table the entire time we're there, the smile on her pale thin lips a substitute
for the Hebrew she cannot speak. In my kindergarten, Yehoshua is the
only one who had grandparents. We all go straight home after supper, but
he must visit them first. Mom keeps pictures of her family in a yellow
wooden box. On her free Saturdays she shows them to me: "This is my
father, this is my mama, these are Dunya and Sarah. This was your grandfather, Avraham," she tries to link us together, her eyes moist. But I feel
no connection with the severe-looking bearded man in the picture, and
Mom does not insist. When children cry they can't speak. With Mom the
tears are added to speech.

Forty years passed before I first made this calculation: Mom was
twenty-nine when she had me. So when I was in the nursery and she
would come home after giving her group their supper, she must have been
thirty-one, thirty-two—good heavens, a young woman. She never played
ball or hopscotch with me, never laughed with me. Eventually I understood that when she came to me at the end of the day her gravity was
purely exhaustion—her love had been drained during the day by a dozen
greedy mouths. The movement's gurus also did the damage. The old family is obsolete, the educationalists proclaimed. We shall create a new family, the education committee told her. Away from mother's apron strings
we shall bring up natural, healthy children, echoed the general meeting.
And she believed everything she was told, as a Hassid believes his rabbi.
But her love looked in through the windows, peered through the cracks,
peasant-like, persistent as crabgrass. Her look, that never wavered through
all my moods and caprices, through all the children's ailments of which I
didn't miss one, solidified as ballast inside me, steadying me amid the
waves. A memory flash: I'm, what—three? four? lying in bed, and Mom is
walking in the dark passage of the children's house. I'm feeling really ill,

sinking slowly into a boundless obscurity. The kibbutz doctor who examined me that afternoon had uttered quietly the word diphtheria and spread out his hands. Mom is pacing up and down in the corridor, unable to sit still. In the dusk her face looks black with sorrow and her hands move spasmodically at her sides, as if struggling with an unseen enemy.

A couple of years ago I was invited by some friends, followers of the method of the American psychologist Harville Hendrix, to watch a video film of one of his workshops. After an hour of explanations, some more persuasive than others, Hendrix asked one of the participants to sit opposite her husband and talk to him as though he were her mother, and say everything she'd always wanted to say but suppressed. At first the woman hesitated, but pretty soon she found her voice and after a few moments broke down and wept uncontrollably. I remembered I'd left something in my car and went out for some air. I knew all the answers, but the child I had been was shaking with sobs and could not speak. All I could get out of him was the strangled cry, *Why, Mom, why, Mom?* I had to take him home and put him to bed, soothed to sleep by Hava Alberstein singing, "On the shore of Kinneret Lake a splendid palace stands, in a wondrous garden filled with trees that no winds shake . . ."

In those far-off years the intense awareness of the absent mother, who appears only to leave again, flew in the face of the kibbutz projects. "A child cannot long for what it has never had, it cannot miss what it has never known," the lecturers at the ideological seminars and the training courses for children's nurses persuaded one another. But memory did not start in the children's house, nor did it end there. The nurses were with us from the moment we rose till after supper, when our parents came to take us to their rooms; they fed us three meals a day, bathed us and put us to bed in the afternoon and at night, and supervised us in the sandbox and playground. Yet when they were reassigned to different work, all that remained of them was a dim memory, acknowledged with an awkward smile when we came across them somewhere in the kibbutz. Memory had an independent life, unmoved by the finest theories. Though one grew up without her, memory pieced together the few contacts, filled in the gaps and composed the image of the absent mother. Though one grew up without a home, memory built up an image of it.

Once I caught cold just before the annual trip in fourth grade, and fell ill. Feeling miserable about missing the trip made my temperature rise higher. Dazed with high fever, I lay that evening on my parents' porch, and Mom suggested that I stay for a few days. It felt strange to lie on Mom's bed in the little room, as the shivering chills thawed and turned into sweet warmth. At ten Father came home from doing the work roster, and was surprised to find me there. I had only ever slept with them once before: one night, when I was three or four years old, and Father was on duty as night watchman, he came into the children's house and I fled into his arms from the terror of the jackals. Now Mom explained that she'd suggested I stay with them because I was ill. Her low voice sounded unusually firm. Then she came in, wished me good night, and drew the curtain that divided the two rooms. In the darkness I heard the sound of the kettle boiling, a teaspoon tinkled, the radio announcer's pedantic voice, a chair being dragged and the shuffle of Father's slippers. These sounds didn't prevent me from falling asleep, and listening to them was like connecting dots to make up a picture. The picture I got was clear enough for me to say to myself, as I dozed off, that I liked the sounds of home, that they were making me sleepy. Strangely enough, as soon as the picture became plain, the sounds duplicated themselves like echoes and turned into a recollection, a dim one to be sure but quite certain, of many other evenings when I did not actually sleep there. When Mom put her head through the curtain and asked if I wanted something to drink, I replied, snug with drowsiness and fever, that she shouldn't worry, I would be better tomorrow.

A Moment's Silence, Please

A.

I spent the 1996 Christmas vacation in Israel, at the bedside of my eighty-six-year-old father in the Harzfeld Geriatric Hospital in Gedera. Hemorrhages in his arms and legs forced the doctors to attach to his shoulders the various tubes that dripped medications into him, and these hung like slack parachute strings over his head. His heart was too weak to clear the uric acid from his legs, which turned red and swollen. His kidneys hardly functioned, and he had difficulty breathing. An unfortunate combination of medications caused him to tremble all over, and his speech was unintelligible. But his practical nature never left him to the end, and his failing hands kept trying to adjust the connection of the tubes into his body. These ceaseless attempts, indicating that inside the unrecognizable body there still lived a clear mind, moved me to pity. My grandfather—it seems strange to refer thus to a man whom I never even saw in a photograph—like many Jews in Bessarabia combined Hassidism with commerce. He died in a typhoid epidemic in Bendery in 1920. My father joined the youth movement Gordonia at sixteen, and remained a socialist all his life. It was socialism that carried him, in March 1937, by bus, truck, and mule cart from the port of Haifa to the movement's first kibbutz, and for nearly half a century sent him at daybreak every morning to the apple orchards for which he was responsible. But his elaborate notions of equality availed him little in his old age, and he could rely only on himself and his tremulous hands to ease his pain. My grandfather had believed that when he

15

died he would return to God's infinite, compassionate being. My father did not know what he expected, and in his sunken eyes lurked the fear of death.

Some twelve years earlier, as we walked towards the Shavuot celebration held on the lawn behind the kibbutz culture hall, my father told me about a member's funeral that had taken place the day before. He said, contemptuously, that the man had clung to the kibbutz and to life even as the cancer devoured him all over. Now he himself was lying on a hospital bed, his body as misshapen as a plasticine figure, and never missed a meal or left anything on his plate. He had no way of knowing the world except as a reflection of himself, and the calculations of profit and loss he had inherited from his father. Afraid of the doctors and of his community members who were waiting for him to die, he used what little energy he had left to raise his head to the spoonfuls of food Mom handed him.

A week after my arrival he recovered his speech and told me with some embarrassment—pouting like an offended child—that when he woke from his afternoon sleep it seemed to him for a moment that it was his mother, Faigeh—who had died at the age of sixty shortly before he left for Israel—but looking older, sitting beside his bed. When he first met Mom she bore no resemblance, with her red cheeks, black hair, and the confident smile that hovered between her thick eyebrows and thrusting chin, to his mother's fallen, pallid face. Now he was astonished to discover that his mother's face continued to age in the face of his eighty-year-old wife, and his weakened eyes discovered the resemblance they had never noticed in youth.

In the evenings, when we left Father, I would take Mom back to the kibbutz. We'd drink tea and talk in low voices, as though there was an invalid in the house. "Father is having a terrible old age," Mom kept repeating, in case I hadn't noticed. In her native small town nobody lived to the advanced age of eighty-six, and she was no longer there when her parents died—the Germans who invaded Bessarabia did not give the Jews an opportunity to examine their life expectancy. She and Father came to the kibbutz as members of a youth movement, and old age seemed to violate the promise implicit in that long membership. She had imagined that the age of eighty would thin her husband's hair and weaken his muscles. She had never imagined that old age meant legs like two immobile, red and purple lumps, buttocks like a punctured inner soccer ball. When she hugged him before we left, she was again astonished by how narrow his shoulders had become, as though deep inside the rugged, sunburnt man a pallid, aged child had always been hiding. For sixty years she had lived with his bitterness and sententious criticisms, accustomed to seeing in him the boy who lost his father at the age of nine, knowing that she would never be rewarded for her patience. She never believed that life was meant to be happy, and life adapted itself to her nunlike patience. When he first fell ill he refused to have strangers take care of him, and though eighty herself, she washed and cleaned him, and was amazed that the pains in her back and pelvis, which had often kept her in bed, simply went away. In the first four years after their first meeting, in her native town of Bricheva, they saw each other at long intervals, and would spend the time before parting in mutual promises and encouragement. Red-eyed, she would shut herself in her room, and he would rally her with assurances that the time to their next meeting would pass quickly. Then it was her turn to comfort and cheer him up, and so on—as though they were tied together by one yearning love which swung wildly between them. When they were finally united in the kibbutz, in 1938, and produced their first child, their love stopped swinging to and fro and settled in her. When his illness freed her from pain, she realized that they had also been allocated a single measure of suffering. She nursed him devotedly, feeding him five times a day to spare his delicate stomach, but his eyes remained querulous and his face took on the pallor of suffering. From habit, she continued to hope that he would recover, and from habit, could not imagine how she would live without him.

Early in January, on the eve of my return to the United States, I went to the hospital for the last time. A three-day beard made my father's face grayer still and his eyes were sunk deeper. He raised his head, pressed my hand feebly, and said, "We'll see each other in the summer, as usual." "As usual," I replied, forcing a smile. He strained his face to respond with a confident, fatherly smile, but the one thing he knew for certain was that this was our last meeting. As I said good-bye again, his face expressed bewilderment and sorrow, as if he had let me down by being old. Mom walked with me to the exit and in the hospital doorway asked glumly, "What if something happens to Father during the semester—will you come?" Outwardly grown up and considerate, I hugged her shoulders, which had greatly shrunken and drooped in the past year, surprised to hear my thoughts coming from her mouth. My heart went out to her grief.

B.

"A moment's silence, please. I've something to say to you," said the school principal. The solemn parade (May Day? The first Day of Independence?) was being held in the square in front of the kibbutz water tower. The members, in short khaki pants and white shirts, are standing on the black earth in three rows forming a big U. It's the first time I see this human U, but it looks perfectly natural to me, and as firm as a field or a hill. "Quiet, please," the principal repeats. One of the big boys is standing on the platform, drumming, and the Israel flag rises slowly on the high water tower. It snaps there in the wind, solemn and dramatic. Sharp cries come from the platform, and all the legs around me are moving as one, separating and stamping on the ground. The earth trembles like the skin of an immense drum.

The principal reads something from a paper in his hand. I let the flag scatter the ringing words high above me, like paper birds. I like standing beside Father's leg. He doesn't have to put me to bed, or to take me for a walk to give Mom a chance to rest, only to stand in place. We are facing the same way. His sunburnt knee rises and falls like an Adam's apple when you swallow.

The principal finishes speaking and folds his papers, and again there are crisp shouts from the platform. The legs around me again separate and stamp hard, pounding the earth drum. I'm not afraid. I feel good and safe beside Father's leg. The ceremony is over and the big U breaks up. The strong lights blazing on either side of the platform make the faces gleam like metal. Everybody's smiling, talking and smiling, standing around smiling. The smile reaches our neighbor Alioshka, as always standing by himself, and rebounds like an echo. In a moment the members will reach up to the faint stars in the sky and hang them on their chests for decoration. Where is Father now? I don't know. Memory has captured him standing beside me, rock steady on the earth drum. As the moments from the earth's shaking pass, so memory too fades away, and soon disappears altogether.

Another moment:

Father is taking me and my big brother Elan to feed the two hares he's raising in a coop near the east fence of the kibbutz. The wind is chasing its tail on the flowering clover field, as far as the olive grove beyond. It's nice, walking with Father, Elan on one side of him and me on the other, and a sense of abundance in the blue air: we have all day ahead of us, as well as the wide field, and I need not return to the kindergarten till lunchtime. It's Saturday today and Father has time for us, and things are all tied together: I to Father and Elan, and the winter rains to the clover, which has grown so high, and the clover to the two golden hares in whose eyes float tiny red dots. There is time and nothing to do, only to walk with Father and Elan, to pluck damp clover and give it to the hares, who shorten the stalks with every twitch of their noses. Everything is quite simple: the hand moving in its natural path, clutching Father's hand or offering clover to the hares, the clover field stirring freely in the breeze, and the hares chewing in time with the movements of their triangular noses. Everything is simple, linked together and comprehended.

A moment's silence, please. On March 15, 1997, I boarded a plane to return to Israel, not knowing if I'd find my father alive still. In the noisy, darkened plane I recalled two wonderful moments I'd had in his company. There may well have been others, but during the long flight my memory was an unruly, unkind child.

What Did You Learn in Kindergarten Today?

A.

During the early thirties my father visited the branches of the Gordonia youth movement in Bessarabia, distributed leaflets of the Jewish National Fund, and thrilled the youngsters with stories about the early kibbutzim. Recruiting new members was easier than he'd expected. After World War I, Bessarabia was annexed to Romania, and it took only a few years for the new government to decide that the Jews were greedily draining the rich country's wealth. The newspapers carried passionate appeals to rid the Romanian people of the Jewish parasites, and young Jews flocked to the Zionist movements which offered solutions to the menace. (Mom's two older sisters were members of *Hashomer Hatzair* and *Poalai Zion*, respectively. When they all came home in the evening and went up to their rooms to sleep, their father would sigh: "I've sent all the parties to bed. Now it's my turn.") At the age of twenty, my father ran the Gordonia branch in his town, and the following year was sent by the movement to organize new branches and strengthen weak ones. He traveled from city to city, from townlet to townlet, bearing the message of the pioneering philosopher from Deganiah. The idea of exchanging a life of poverty and hard work among the gentiles for a plain laboring life among the Arabs in the faraway Land of Israel was entrancingly simple, and the youngsters who listened to it were too immature to realize that putting the mystic-philosopher's ideas into practice was doomed to failure. Swaying to and fro, my father expounded the thirteen principles of his movement, stroking his nonexistent beard like a rabbinical scholar expounding those other thirteen principles.

My father did not turn on his children the charm that had worked wonders with his young disciples. Only when visitors filled the house on a Saturday or a holiday did his tired tortoise gaze suddenly liven up, he would slap his knee or touch his listeners' shoulders, jumping from story to story. His excellent memory retained anecdotes and Hassidic tales he'd heard from his father, which he wove into his own stories. Normally he returned from work in the apple orchard when daylight failed, took a shower, and tried to rest a little before supper. After the meal he would stay in the dining hall to prepare for the next day's work, in the midst of the cluster that surrounded the work-roster man. The time assigned to his children was the gap between his shower and supper. He would lie down, cover his face with a sheet or a newspaper, and we would walk around on tiptoe, as in a sickroom. We clearly felt that we were a nuisance to him, and he was a burden to us. The apple varieties, Delicious, Nonpareil, even the delicate Galia Beauty, reached the Tel Aviv market safely, despite all the hardships of fruit picking, sorting, and packaging. But how to touch us, his children, that he didn't know. On stormy nights he would rush out, like a true farmer, to ensure that his tender saplings were unhurt by the blast. My vocabulary was still quite small, and I didn't yet know the words Zionism, Socialism, or Building a Secure Home for the Jewish People. But I did recognize Nehemiah's footsteps when he ran to Avigdora's bed, to hide in it from the thunderstorm.

For some obscure reason, I wanted my father to teach me to shave. He seemed taken aback, surprised perhaps that I still expected him to act like a parent, promised to show me how, then forgot. (Strangely, I can only remember his look. I don't remember where I made the request, only his puzzled expression, and now I also recall that he was wearing glasses; yes, he looked up and peered at me under the frames.)

He did, however, occasionally share with us some of the skills he'd acquired on the roads: you can soften the bits of newspaper we use in the toilet by twisting them like a corkscrew between our hands, or: runny snot is a great ointment for mild burns. Seeing the blisters on my palms after using a hoe, he advised me that the best cure for them was urine, and urged me to try it out at once. In later days, when the economic state of the kibbutz improved, he showed me how to split a toothpick in two. This poor folks' wisdom, the lore of the old townlets—what have I to do with it today? Yet these are things I recall to his credit.

One of the few lessons he taught me was how to use a rifle. Not long before the Suez War, a house at the far end of the kibbutz was blown up by infiltrators from the Jordanian border, and the watch on the kibbutz fences was stepped up. When my father's turn came to act as night watchman, he brought home a long English rifle and propped it in the corner of the bathroom. During the Sabbath-eve supper I asked him to teach me to shoot, and to my surprise he agreed. He would be free the next day and would teach me. My imagination was on fire. Before falling asleep I saw myself, slim and silent, passing from one guard post to the next, the rifle in my hand being both a field glass and firearm. I got up early the next day. Father, who had been on duty that night, slept till midday. A few minutes before lunch he called me over, and sitting on the porch he showed me how to load and unload the gun. We didn't go to the woods, didn't set up targets, and didn't shoot. "Is that all?" "What did you think?" he grinned uncomfortably. This is how the shooting lesson remains in my memory: Father tired and unshaved, his instructions squeezed between making the bed and going to lunch, and the smell of rifle grease blending with the odor of a semidigested night snack. I remember that lesson to his credit too.

And yes, he also taught me to plant. The cypress I planted on my first *Tu Bishvat* ceremony leaned sideways after I watered it. Father came to my aid: he pulled the stick-like cypress out of the hole in the ground, showed me how to steady the sapling by pressing down the soil around the roots, then adding layer of crumbled earth on top, to enable air and water to filter down. When, a week later, I planted a big squill bulb near the house I followed his instructions to the letter. (A few days later I took it out of the ground to see if it had sprouted roots.) In those days there was a little chicken coop behind our children's house, and I soon learned to recognize the loud, excitable quacking that proclaimed a laid egg. I peered through the cracks into the laying boxes and watched in amazement how the egg was expelled from the hen's body and how the red orifice from which it popped out opened and shut a couple of times afterwards, like a mouth after a yawn. While watching, I cut my finger on a nail that protruded from the back of the coop, and before the red blood welled out of the white flesh I stared in fascination into myself, unconscious of the pain. This desire to observe life in action through the surface of the earth or the skin would remain with me in various forms for years to come. When I first had a house of my own, it became a greenhouse for houseplants. I still need to see things growing nearby, striking roots, putting out new leaves. ("I left the first lemons for you to pick," my wife said to me last May, when I arrived for the summer holidays. I smiled sheepishly—she already knew all my weaknesses. The two lemon trees in the garden of our new home in Evven-Yehuda had produced three large, asymmetrical lemons, as though the young branches had yet to learn the art of producing a proper elliptical shape.) And to this day, when I plant a flower or a tree, or transfer a plant from pot to pot, I remember my father's sunburnt hands showing me how to plant a cypress tree, or stroking a cluster of apples with the affection he reserved for his trees.

B.

When I was in kindergarten, I had a passion for pigeons. Elan was generally more moderate than I, but I succeeded in infecting him with this craze. He helped me to build a dovecote on a pole opposite our house. One day we saw a pigeon brooding on the roof of one of the wooden shacks, and Elan suggested that when the fledglings were old enough, we would take them to serve as the nucleus of our own flock. We went quietly to the shack every few days; I'd climb on Elan's shoulders and then on to the roof, and report on the situation in the nest. I soon noticed that when the female dove was sitting on the eggs, she stirred uneasily and glared at me with her orange button eyes, till I was within arm's reach. When the male was brooding, he would take off as soon as he heard our footsteps down below. He would vanish behind the seed store, and we avoided each other's eyes, as if we'd been caught out.

Gordonia Hulda

A.

My father's father died when he was nine, and he had to go to work after primary school. My mind never connected this piece of information with my father's massive, sunburnt image, either because the few stories I heard him tell described his days as the organizer of Gordonia in his town and the movement's emissary, or because it is hard for a child to regard his father as an orphan. It had never struck me that Mom came from a prosperous family, which sent its children to the best schools and music academies, while Father had to work for a living from an early age. Both the wealth and the poverty belonged in a faraway reality, totally unrelated to our children's house and dining hall. The kibbutz, which gave my parents the same work clothes and fed them the same food on the sticky formica-topped tables as everyone else, created an illusion of equality. At the age of fifty-three I flew home to part from a man who had been a proud Gordonian throughout his life and mine, and found an orphaned boy. We buried him in the Hulda cemetery, surrounded by the children of the poor who had flocked to Gordonia. How could I have known: someone, moved by a mad Christian logic, had tried to turn hunger and orphanhood into gold dust.

B.

Sunday evening, the sixth day of the mourning week. The room in which we received visitors was crowded. Some of Elan's old classmates were sitting with him on the sofa, and Mom was surrounded by many of her former charges. I vacated my chair and went into the bedroom. Last December Mom had asked Elan, Dinah, and me to take the books Father had accumulated. She did not feel up to cleaning the place and dusting the books. Now the empty bookcases sported only a few family photographs. Here we were all together, in black and white: Mom, Father, two sons, and a daughter (Elan and I with mustaches! I'd clean forgotten). For a moment I felt a twinge of longing for the family we might have been. Leaning against the wall in magnificent isolation was the volume "Gordonia," published a few years ago by the movement's archive in Hulda. None of us cared to take it, and Mom didn't have the heart to dispose of it. I opened the book and began to leaf through it, but my eyes slid over the text and could not take it in. The one paragraph stood out from the mass: "The movement of Hashomer Hatzair, launched a few years before Gordonia, started out as a movement of young students. Thousands of ordinary, working young people, enslaved from childhood by hardships, debasing circumstances, without education or decent labor, were left outside the parameters of the Zionist youth movement. Those young people who did not manage to attend secondary school or academies did not make it into the youth movement either. This was the reality which gave rise to Gordonia." So the young people of Hashomer Hatzair were the sons and daughters of prosperous families who could afford to send them to secondary school, while the Gordonians were the working or unemployed youngsters, the marginal youth of the townlets—I translated to myself, in disbelief, the words of Pinhas Lavon, as though I had switched from language to language, from the familiar kibbutz to another one. I hurried to the front room.

None of Elan's former classmates knew that Gordonia had been primarily a movement of working, uneducated young people. I questioned one after the other about the economic circumstances of the families their parents had left behind them in Europe. The question drew embarrassed grins. "Your brother's turning our parents into underprivileged young people," Yehudit, an old classmate, said to Elan, smiling. Her mother had been my group's nurse in kindergarten, and I knew her father well from my years of working in the olive grove. I recalled their heavy, impassive features and wondered how I could have been so blind for so long. "Enough," Elan begged me, grinning in a way that reminded me how much I loved him when I was a child. "You're upsetting our guests."

What did we know when we were children? Nothing about Gordonia.

The name itself wore a dull sheen, like a coin from another era. The strangeness that divided us from the adults—their awkward Hebrew, their townlet humor, their old-time gray caps and jackets we used to borrow for our Purim parties—made for some mockery and giggling, but did not extinguish the sheen. By contrast, we thought we knew all there was to know about Hulda. We were in second grade when Ozer Huldai, our school principal, made us learn by heart Yehuda Karni's poem, "The Huldaites," composed after the Arab destruction of the settlement in 1929. As he read it to us a white droplet moved across his lower lip from corner to corner, his right hand conducted the beat, and his whole body swayed with it: "The Huldaites our nation did not shame: / A brave night it was, cold yet flaming hot. / Ablaze the copse, / laid waste the courtyard. / Will Judah's lion cubs retreat from Hulda?" The old-fashioned pronunciation of the name Hulda made it rhyme with Judah, conferring an ancient honor upon the twenty-four brave defenders. The purple passage seemed to set Hulda apart from the other kibbutzim and filled us with pride. The squat children's houses, the dining hall, the uneven pavements covered with thick mud in winter—they all wore a halo of glory, and one could only wish that everyone, the Tel Avivians and the members of other kibbutzim, could see and admire it. We were princes. Though we never talked about it, we rejoiced in our aristocratic status. The following year, at the wedding of Eitana and Yossi, Ozer stood on the stairs of the culture hall and read the kibbutz's first marriage scroll. He would declaim those phrases on the same spot and in the same enthusiastic intonation at every subsequent wedding, and the gathering, shiny eyed, would murmur with him: "This scroll is a memorial and testimony to the day of their marriage and the rejoicing of Hulda, our communal settlement—this Hulda which was devastated in 1929, despite its heroic resistance against the Arab marauders, and was rebuilt in 1931. This Hulda, from which the Army of Israel went forth to smite our enemies and breach the siege of Jerusalem . . ." The highfalutin phrases went well with our freshly ironed clothes and the festive atmosphere, raising Hulda aloft like a torch. The members attended seminars and reported their impressions in the kibbutz paper, discussed the ideals of equality and communalism, and bandied concepts and ideas in the dining hall, making them as tangible as the tables and bread loaves. Who could have guessed that most of them had been poverty-stricken children, apprenticed to carpenters, tailors, and cobblers, working youths to whom Gordonia brought glad tidings as Christ's promise did to the poor of Jerusalem?

"What did Father do after primary school?" Mom echoed my question. "Well, you know he had to help support the family after his father died. They got him a job working for a tailor who used to be his father's friend." Indeed, on rainy days he worked in the kibbutz clothing store, sewing and mending clothes. He told me more than once that after his father's sudden death, his elder brother had to give up his studies at secondary school, and whenever he ran into his former classmates he hung his head in shame. He demonstrated his brother's lowered head and shamed expression, but only now I understood his roundabout narrative. It was not difficult to imagine him gazing enviously at the boys from the gymnasium and the Zionist dream they nurtured at their clubs. Gordonia enabled him to share in the dream, but it did not free him from the insult of his poverty, from his envy of the well-off and the educated. Now, at long last, I had a key to his grumbling hatred, the hatred of a man who does not like himself, a furious, unforgiving hate, feeding upon real or imaginary offenses. To the end of his days he felt like a poor relative in the world and nursed his grievances as a miser nurses his gold. Having to choose between attending a wedding to which he was invited late or staying at home, he always chose the latter.

Nevertheless, on the few occasions I accompanied him to Tel Aviv he carried himself proudly, bearing his kibbutz membership like a sign of the elect. Hulda was the first kibbutz founded by Gordonia, and the thousands of movement members who remained in Europe breathed down its neck with pride. Even after the establishment of the state of Israel, its members regarded themselves as an avant-garde, the spearhead of the Labor movement, the essence of the difference between Israeli society and all other societies. They had contacts in the party and the government, and when it was necessary to obtain a larger ration of water or permission to sell more eggs, they always knew whom to approach. Unfortunately—my childhood passed quickly before my mind's eye and I could hardly keep up with my impressions—this sense of superiority did not relieve the tailor's apprentice's distress. It was not as though a sense of inferiority was turned into its opposite—the two existing side by side. And in the gap between them Father stored hatred, nursed rages, and brooded on slights. This gap thickened his skin when he spoke to other people, and became thin as silk when they spoke to him.

"I didn't have a problem with him," Elan said when the last visitors left. "He simply wasn't a part of my life." Of the three of us, he alone has Father's rugged, sunburnt physique. Dinah and I have Mom's freckled, easily flushed skin. "Look, the amount of time Father gave us was just enough to pass on his nervousness, his insecurity, and his sensitive stomach, thanks very much. But at least none of us inherited his capacity for hate. I have friends who tell me that they miss their dead parents. Well, that's one problem we don't have to deal with." Dinah made no attempt to hide her resentment. Her big eyes, like Mom's in her youth, studied me across the table. "Say you're right, but why couldn't he just once put me on his knees, just once stroke my head? It's totally irrelevant now if I forgive him or not." Under her black mane she's once again a little girl who keeps asking Mom, Elan, and me if we love her. And who is speaking from my mouth if not the scrawny kid who's trying to please his parents and teachers so as to win a little sense of security? It suddenly came to me that my children too complain that I left them when they were too small. The family picture has expanded and a lump of sorrow weighs on my breast: orphanhood and absence and selfishness have duplicated themselves like some sly DNA.

C.

I left Mom with Dinah and Elan and hurried to the flat the kibbutz had given us for the shivah. The sorrow for Father's death was beginning to weigh on me more than I'd expected. I took out my laptop and went over all the files in the folder "Parents." In January 1995 I was invited to spend six months at the Centre for Jewish Studies at Oxford. The center is located in a beautiful seventeenth-century manor in the village of Yarnton, not far from Oxford. In my first letters from Yarnton I told my parents about the lovely English countryside, and the joy of being paid to devote oneself to one's love, namely, writing. My father replied that my letter had prompted him to think harder than ever—might not a man who is feeling content be more willing to forgive parents who had sinned against him by treating him too casually when he was a child. He apologized for the fact that he and Mom had tacitly allowed their children to serve as guinea pigs

for educators rich in imagination and poor in experience. The only justification, he wrote, was that they had acted in error, not in malice. His
letter was, as usual, full of spelling mistakes, but the biblical phrase "He
who confesses his faults and gives them up will find mercy" was written
correctly.

Finally I found the right file: Yarnton, 2.16.95. I was pleased to find that
the temperate English landscape—the woolly pastures, the hedgerows,
which were beginning to wake up and fill with shiny green coins, as
though rumors of spring reached them all at the same time—had made
me hypocritical and generous:

"Father, thanks for your long letter. In one of her recent letters Mom
told me about Elan and his wife, who were travelling in South America,
and that Dinah was coming to visit you, and added, in the same breath,
'Here the cotton harvest has begun, and we hope it will be finished before
the rains come.' I said to myself, here is a woman of eighty, not in good
health, whose legs no longer carry her on afternoon walks through the
kibbutz and its fields, yet she still follows all that's happening in the kibbutz. And so, after reporting all the family doings, she adds a line about
the cotton, as though cotton was also a cherished family member. And I
said to myself: these people, who had had no connection with agriculture,
who forced themselves to become farmers, because they believed that that
was the way to develop the country and to develop with it, and did this
hour after hour, day after day, for sixty long years. As for the mistakes that
were made in the early years, I have long ago forgiven them, and it is time
you also forgave yourselves. So, until next time, warm regards to Mom,
and to the cotton, which as you know, I also remember fondly."

Four Eyes, Two Mouths

A.

Eleven o'clock at night. Tuesday, the first day of the shivah. The last of the visitors have left, Dinah and Elan have gone about their business, leaving Raheli and me with Mom. "What shall I do now, all alone? What shall I do, all alone?" Mom's voice expressed despair and wonder. When we thought we'd succeeded in calming her down, her grief found other routes. "Avremalé was sick with the flu and was running a high fever. I was so worried, I slept in his children's house. In the middle of the night he woke up and, in a hoarse voice full of phlegm, called his nurse. Do you know any other place where a child wakes in the night and calls not his mother, but the nurse?" she asked my wife disconsolately.

Waving her hand in front of her face, as though to dismiss her lamentation, Mom said, "Go to sleep, son, you must be still exhausted from your flight." She was trying to resume the heroic role she had played for so long. I rose to go and she kissed my arm, then wiped the trace of her lips. Dinah came back, and my wife and I went to spend the night in a nearby house. I remembered exactly who had occupied each of the apartments in the veterans' houses. But most of the founding members had already passed away, and their homes were occupied by outside tenants, attracted by the low kibbutz rents. Yuval, who was in charge of letting the empty apartments, had offered us, as an old-time kibbutz gesture, one of them for the duration of the shivah. In this apartment everything is not quite: a not-quite refrigerator, a not-quite double bed, not-quite pillows and blankets. Outside, rusty iron rods show through the cracked walls. My parents' house was renovated last summer, after lengthy delays, but the cracks are opening up again. In any case, you don't look a gift home in the mouth.

"Pity your mother is no longer very mobile," said my wife. "It's hard for her that you're all so far away." "Between us and the kibbutz, they chose the kibbutz," I said. "I cried for my nurse, and other children cried for my mother, who was their nurse." "Yes, but you only need to hear the way she says your name to know how dear you are to her," Raheli said, trying to understand. "Well, you can't give the best love and care in the world for half an hour, then disappear for the rest of the day. And that's how it was, day after day, year after year. Her love and her best intentions only created openings which in those days were not supposed to exist here." Thinking about Mom's grief and her loneliness opened old wounds. Lying on the skimpy mattress, with the rustling of the loquat and pecan trees outside, I told my wife a bedtime story. When I began to speak I saw a single picture, but its setting soon became clear, the way a line from an old song drags along other lines that you did not know were still stored in your memory.

B.

The club in my hand hits the tennis ball exactly in the center, at its full momentum. The ball flies off and away, crosses the boundary of the main lawn—in a moment it will disappear like a bird behind the first row of houses beside the dining hall. Hiding a pleased grin, I run to the first base, then the second, and complete the circle. It'll soon be seven o'clock, but the game of rounders is still going strong. Meanwhile, waiting for my turn, I sprawl on the grass. Not far from me sits Yigal, watching the game and repeating, thick-lipped, the players' cries of encouragement and disappointment. His big, horsy head follows every flight of the ball. "A fine strike," he says to me, laughing aloud, trying to make friends, though I'm in fifth grade and he's in seventh.

Amatzia is looking for a partner to join the game. "Come, have a go," he says to Yigal. "Oh no," Yigal smiles sheepishly. "Come on!" Amatzia urges him, the stare of his blue eyes more persuasive than his words. Yigal rises, fearing a trap, and walks behind Amatzia towards the players. "Hey, are you kidding?" the boys shout at Amatzia, protesting against the intrusion of such unequal forces into the game. Yigal looks around quickly, offering everyone his frightened grin, momentarily trying on Amatzia's self-confident expression that says, who're you to say who can play and who can't?

"How're you doing, Igloo?" Moshe, from my brother's class, slaps him on the top of his head. Taken by surprise, Yigal recoils, swallows his smile. "What did I do to you?" he protests, offended, still clinging to the illusion of equality—it's just a mistake, he'll soon fix it. "How're you doing, Eskimo?" says Shimon, cuffing him on the head. "Hey boys, Igloo's here," cries Noam, bumping him from behind with his knee, and shoves him with his tanned, hairy arms towards the dining hall. Yigal's big face contorts as if he's about to throw up, and his sunken eyes grow moist with the hurt. His mouth twitches, then he bursts into tears. Goddamn, always the same thing. Not enough brains to take care of himself, only to get hurt. Disconsolate, hopeless sobs shake his broad back as he lurches along the pavement to his parents' house. The groups re-form on the grass, but the pleasure in the game is gone. While Yigal disappears among the veterans' houses, his offended tears make my eyes prickle, like a wave of nausea at the sight of a child throwing up.

The game is over. Darkness settles thickly on the trees, like a flock of crows. Over the hilly vineyards a moon with a pale girl's face sets out on its nightly rounds. A persistent sprinkler diffuses the light that falls on it from my parents' window. "What's wrong?" Mom asks. She has just come home from work, her face still freckled with tiny drops of sweat. "Nothing. We played rounders." "So why the long face? You win some, you lose some." "I didn't lose," I retort, clutching my triumph. "What is it then?" she insists. "Nothing," I reply angrily, then describe Yigal's hurt expression. "Always the same thing! It's not your business. He's got parents, he's got teachers and a nurse," she argues heatedly, as though I'd chosen to make it my business. "You must learn to pull yourself together," she pleads. She feels me all over with the soft touch of her eyes, checking for damage. One evening, when I was in kindergarten, I had toothache, but there was nothing against pain in the house. "Here, try to chew on the hurt," Mom said, taking an unexpected chewing gum out of her apron. The sweetness intensified the pain. "We'll have to wait for the doctor's appointment that you've got tomorrow," she said, covering her face with her hand. Evening fell and in the dusk four blue eyes shone brightly, as if tears could be passed from one to the other. That's how it is with us. Every pain of mine has four eyes, every sigh of hers two throats. She doesn't read her brother's letters from Russia to Elan or to Dinah. Only to me. She reads them in a low voice, red-eyed, and her sigh pierces me as if I were skinless. Now goddamn it, I must pull myself together. I have homework to do. I've nothing more to say to her.

Crowding

Imagine a group of people in a not very big house, who have committed themselves to sleeping together, eating together, bathing together, and toiling on the land together. In the early days they're unconscious of the pitfall, because they are pioneers, they are realizing a dream, and the neighboring Arabs, malaria, and typhoid fever are enough to worry about. The ancestral land yields wheat and olives and milk. You can't know what it feels like to return home in the evening, sit on the shadowed concrete steps, and pull off your work boots, knowing that you've picked a quarter-tonne of apples, and the picking movements linger in the weary body the way a car's vibration lingers in the body after a long journey, like a mild intoxication. The work does not give them a new heart, but it does sometimes produce a countryman's contentment, a countryman's joy and honest sleep. On feast days there is such rejoicing that the heart seems to melt, and even on working days, after supper, before or after the children's bedtime, there is laughter and idle chat in the corners of the dining hall. An old comradeship envelops the inhabitants. Some go away on various business, and when they come back they revel in it as in comfortable old shoes. And you can't help envying them, because their labor is "covered with light as with a garment": they're pioneers, they're Gordonians, they came to Eretz Israel to build and be rebuilt . . .

They are Gordonians, but most of them received Gordon's ideas from their leaders. And the latter never told them that Gordon had emphasized the importance of a good distance between houses: "And when you shall build your house, take care not to multiply its rooms, but pay attention to this—that there should be no barrier between it and the space of the world, the life of the world. That at all times when you dwell in your house, when you rise or lie down to rest, you shall be wholly within that space, within that life. And have a care to put a distance between one house and the next—a goodly distance, which will not rob or hide from any house its portion in this world."

In the early years there was a good deal of movement in the crowded house, men and women trading one corner for another, changing occupations. And then everything stopped still: the crowded sphere pushed everyone into their final pigeonhole. The driver would remain a driver, the dairyman would remain a dairyman, the teacher a teacher; the unmarried person would remain unattached, would linger in the dining hall after supper, communing with a cigarette. The woman who loved a leader of the party would remain in love with him even after he left the place, and would never marry. From month to month the eyes hardened, glazed over, became impervious. The sense of survival whispered that in such close proximity one must not respond to every moan, because one's capacity to respond was barely sufficient for one's spouse and a handful of close friends. And so from month to month, from year to year, faces grew harder and more somber, like tree trunks beside a busy street (think of the ficus trees we saw on Rothschild Boulevard on our way to Habimah Theater). They grunt good morning or good evening to one another without turning their heads, much like discarded lovers turning an aggrieved back to each other, as if to compel a fulfillment of promises made when love still blossomed. They sweep a hollow, unfocused gaze over the hollow people in the dining hall, and only when the eyes encounter a friend do they regain their vision. You won't find in this house the bright, confident looks of independent village farmers who meet in the milking parlor after the evening milking, hide their friendship behind crude jibes, exchange views on current events, or boast about improvements they've made in their cowshed or orange grove.

Year by year, the skin grows tougher. Naftali L. arrived at the end of the war. A blow from a German soldier's rifle had deafened his ear, and his speech sounds broken and distorted. For a while he worked in the potato fields, but kept losing his place. Again and again he asked which was his row. His blurred speech turned "row" into "zho," and before the week was out he was nicknamed "My zho," or "Myzh" for short. He begged to be given his name back. He wrote an agitated plea in the kibbutz paper, but even the printed words, free of his comical accent, were of no avail. The members' children and grandchildren know him only as Myzh, and have no idea that he had a different name when he arrived. Yet they are here in the name of intimacy and sharing, and in their councils, conventions, and seminars they proclaim that the goal of the community is the individual, that the size of the community must be restricted, so as to preserve mutual responsibility, help, and respect. They are here in the name of the human being's daily reopening unto himself, to his comrades, to the fields and the stars, in the name of the return to nature, to its flow and emergence, which know no framework and no barrier—all the concepts they received from A. D. Gordon and Pinhas Lavon and their apostles. They walk down the paths of the kibbutz on their way to work, to the children's houses and the communal showers, like monks intent upon their rituals and prayers in the hope that sanctity will enter their hearts, but sanctity never comes.

Years later, Amos Oz, living in this place, would write stirring stories about the jackals who bare their teeth by night, driven by powerful desires, who gnaw at the vision that brought the people here. But the jackals are not the misfortune of this house, nor the repressed urges—it is the love that was extinguished by overcrowding. The simple fact remains that for untold ages desire assured procreation, and mother's love assured survival. In the thousands of years of human history, mother's love expanded to include expressions of affection and compassion for a man, for a sick mother. The objects of this love stretched lines of longing and words between the tents, built a fence around them, supporting the tribe the way a nest supports the eggs. You have to be blind not to see that love and compassion and kindness are as natural to us today as urges and desires (think of the warmth that fills us, like an inward caress, when we yield to our impulse of kindness. Remember how happy you were last summer, when you were able to help out your cousin when she fell ill in Rome and had to fly home sooner?—you practically danced for joy).

Ten years ago I was invited to lecture in this house. Old age had faded the deep tan I remembered on the faces of the kibbutz members, whitened their lips, and revealed the shopkeepers' expression of their parents, the very expression they had escaped from half a century before, when they came here to create a kibbutz and a homeland. It broke my heart to see these old people, who did not say a word to each other (how their furrowed features softened and opened up when they spoke to me, how their eyes brightened). They were humanity's finest dream in this century, the most consistent attempt to forget humanity's inglorious origins. Every morning for decades they rose early to adapt themselves to the dream that had brought them here. And again I saw that forty, fifty years in one house did not create a wonderful comradeship, but hostile, silent elbows. This way of life, designed for saints and angels, detracted from their humanity. Not the baying of lusts by night brought them down, but the love and kindness, the openness, trust and compassion which toughened along with their faces and thickened with their skin. I sat with them with an aching heart: how they were misled, misguided from the outset.

Cultivators

"Behold, the days come, saith the Lord, that the plowman shall overtake the reaper, and the treader of grapes him that soweth seed; and the mountains shall drop sweet wine, and all the hills shall melt." Zalman read the biblical verses in measured, solemn tones, like a man who knows that the words refer to him. Sheftel's slow, portentous voice answered him from the other end of the dining hall: "Speak unto the children of Israel and say unto them: When ye come into the land which I give unto you, and shall reap the harvest thereof, then ye shall bring a sheaf of the first fruits of your harvest [unto the priest]." It was the Passover Seder, and the gathering, seated at tables arranged in a vast U around the walls, raised the third glass of wine. Zalman and Sheftel's traces of foreign accent caressed the words like a soft cloth polishing ancient silver, made the windows sparkle and gave the light a golden glow.

Harvest and vintage, bushel and scythe, furrow, first fruits and husbandry. The voices lifted in song at Passover, Pentecost, and *Tu Bishvat* reveled in the festive words, and the speakers set them like jewels in their speech. On ordinary workdays these same words, taken from the Bible and from the poems of Bialik and Rahel, gazed down on us from the decorative slogans that hung on the walls of the kindergartens and classrooms.

The wooden cabin that was my first home faced east, toward the barbed wire fence of the kibbutz and the open fields beyond it. Behind them sprawled the evergreen mass of the olive grove, fringed by an avenue of palm trees that led to the woods, its fronds touching the clouds. In the summer I could see the field workers returning at sundown, scythes in their brown hands, wheat dust delineating their facial creases. They walked in a single file, like members of a chivalrous order carrying their families' escutcheons. Sometimes I saw from afar a man walking in the field, holding a bag of seed in one hand while his other hand reached in and scattered, reached in and scattered, the broadcast movements expressing promise and endless assurance. And Hanoch would come back from the pasture, the flock of sheep wending its way behind him through the rusty gate, while the setting sun turned the column of dust to gold.

Shepherd, husbandman, plowman, vintner, yeoman. Beyond the bare walls of the children's house, beyond the terrors of the night, lay a different, mysterious reality, and these were openings that led into it.

My father was always the chief speaker at the family table, but when he fell ill he lost his self-confidence and his urge to speak. In August 1955, when I came to take my leave of him and Mom at the end of the summer vacation, he was already chair-bound, and sat passively, staring into space. Mom gave him supper and he ate slowly, chewing with a joyless, old man's greed. When he finished eating he sat on and stared. Only when Mom started to talk about the kibbutz's economic predicament did he become alert. He had always been concerned with calculations of profit and loss. The word "remunerative" was always on his lips, and I noticed that he was pronouncing the letter "r" with the soft liquid sound of his native tongue. He expounded to me the costs of growing avocados and cotton, as against the price the kibbutz obtained for these crops, and complained: "So what's left for the cultivator?" The word "cultivator" sounded like an unexpected caress. "Come vintners, cultivators, shake your cymbals!" sang the choir at the start of the first-fruits ceremonies. And Mom, forty years younger, sang "Look down from thy holy habitation," and the breeze carried her clear soprano to the wheat fields in front of us, where it wafted away on the rippling corn. Now a group of young girls walking innocently to the well is surrounded by a band of shepherds dressed in pelts. The girls overcome their alarm and soon they're dancing with the shepherds, each pair spinning around, joined by their smile. Then other girls come up on the stage, which is edged with rolls of hay, to do the dance of the priestesses. Their white dresses glow against their wheat-colored suntan, their eyes are wide open, as though they're listening to a melody the rest of us can't hear. Blushing a little, aware of their beauty, they turn slowly, like sorceresses, their arms holding up invisible sheaves—they seem to be offering their youth to the four winds. The audience is sitting all around on bundles of straw, amid festive decorations and slogans. The biblical verses ringing in the afternoon breeze turn the prickly straw into bricks of gold. If we're patient, we shall see Boaz and Ruth coming in from the field, some of us will speak to them in their language, and the rest will look on, smiling proudly. In the meantime, Father assesses in a low voice the value of the first fruits which the workers in the sheepfold, the dairy, and the poultry coops are bringing up on the stage, and the value of a day's work in each of these industries. A born tradesman, he never took a penny for himself, even when the merchants offered him huge sums just to come with them—they would take him and bring him back, how long could it take?—and give them an expert's estimate how many tonnes of fruit they could expect from an apple orchard they were thinking of buying. A tradesman like his father, he still spoke of cultivators, plowmen, and yeomen, the lost gem-words of my childhood. The shiver of longing and sorrow that went through me spread over him. For a moment all was forgiven, overlooked.

Death in a Clown's Cap

A.

Thursday, the third day of the shivah. Mom's contemporaries don't try to console her. They take her in their withered arms, nod with resignation, and advise her to accept: "That's the way it is." "That's the way it is," Mom practices the phrase. The kibbutz, they tell me, red-eyed, is no longer what it was: all the services have been privatized, the dining hall is only open for lunch, the last Passover Seder was celebrated by each family separately, and only at Purim did the young people organize some kind of party. "When we arrived, applicants for membership were selected," says Shimon, who worked with Father for years in the orchards. "Not everyone was accepted. Now the children leave immediately after military service. Now we get couples from the city, people who've never even heard Gordon's name. Those who can't manage in the city because of their children or money problems come to us. Then they act like they built the kibbutz, like they're doing us a favor by keeping us here." "The economic situation is so bad, I can't even get the money that's due to me out of the treasurer. On the other hand, you get paid for the duty rota. You take your turn in the kitchen, or as a driver—here's fifty shekels remuneration," complained Fruma in a voice cracked by old age and cigarettes. "That's the way it is," Mom says quietly. Two weeks before she gave birth to me, she heard that her parents and three brothers perished in Transnistria, where the Jews of Bessarabia had been herded by the Nazis. For two weeks she wept as she tried to think of names that would recall as many of their names as possible. But she was young and the kibbutz was young, Elan was four, and her belly was heavy with me in it. A week after I was born

41

she named me after her father. "That's the way it is," she says now, more than half a century later, defeated.

"You remember the singing and dancing in the dining hall at festivals and weddings?" I ask my sister. "Since leaving, I've danced at a number of parties, and I always felt it was a feeble imitation of the real thing. I don't have to tell you that there was a valuable quality about it, a feeling that we were special and wonderful, maybe not each one individually, but all of us together. I mean, as children we each had problems of our own, but when we were singing and dancing we were first of all Israelis, first of all kibbutz children, and this togetherness was wonderful. Wasn't it worth everything? We'll never be young again, but I'd give anything to experience that unity one more time. I often dream about those days. I often weep in those dreams, from sheer longing."

Lying beside the television I see the latest kibbutz paper, which informs me that the communal Friday night supper has been abolished. "*Response:* I cannot prevent the breaking up of the kibbutz or the privatization of the food," writes Comrade Yohanan. "I am deeply sorry about the cancellation of the Sabbath supper in the dining hall. I remember it as always a festive occasion, the gathering of all the members around the laid tables, and sometimes a short ceremony of *kiddush* and reading the weekly portion.

"I accept the decree with profound regret. There are economic reasons for leaving the special supper to the family circle. The trouble is, of course, that there are some single people who are not always invited to join a family.

"I have no complaints to make about the quality of the food and the way it is served in the dining hall. Nor is it a matter of convenience—the preparation of the food and the washing up—only an emotional reaction and a longing for the atmosphere of the past which will not return."

I find the writer's defeated tone, his awareness that there is no remedy, deeply moving. I also recall with fondness the Sabbath-eve suppers, the dining hall agleam with the white shirts, the shining faces, and the glimmer of oily droplets on the surface of the noodle soup.

The next day I visit the Gordonia archive and ask to see the marriage scroll that was inscribed here. By tradition, the last couple to get married was given the scroll to keep, and passed it ceremoniously to the next couple. None of the workers in the archive can remember who has it now.

"It's years since there's been a wedding here," admits Avigdora, my only classmate to remain in the kibbutz. "But I'll find it, if it matters to you."

B.

My father died on the eve of Purim. The funeral was put off for two days, to enable me to get here in time. The Purim celebrations were held as planned.

The first death that I recall was that of the father of my classmate Yehoshua, who died of a heart attack when we were in third grade. His death silenced the kibbutz for a week: the radios were all turned off and the children did not have their regular music lessons on the recorder and violin. The weekly movie—normally held on Tuesdays—was canceled. When I left the kibbutz, in the sixties, death was still a rare and imposing visitor. In the years that followed I came to recognize Mom's slight hesitation after she said my name on the telephone, meaning that she was about to inform me of the death of another kibbutz member. In the past year the tone of her voice changed. Last December, when I drove her back from the hospital where my father was lying, she named four members who had recently died. She smiled with resignation as she said this. Like the last leaves falling from the branches, the remaining founder members were passing away.

The notice about my father's death was hung on the notice board near the dining hall, not far from the announcement about the Purim parties. When Yehoshua's father died, a cloud of mourning hung over the dining hall and the kibbutz paths, and pricked the eyes like the smoke from the kitchen ovens on cold winter days. Now death wore a clown's cap.

Observing Hands

Possible Memories: A Note on First-Person Narratives

The caresses—what do they remind him of, those intense, desperate caresses on his wife's arm that first spring of their acquaintance in her native town of Bricheva. He finished the lunch she had been feeding him, lay his head back on the pillow and closed his eyes. She stroked the shriveled hand that lay on top of the hospital sheet. Those long caresses, in the spring of 1935, on arms newly bared after a long winter, recalled a hazy picture which almost reached his consciousness but dissolved before he could focus on it. He ruminated on the movement of his palm on the freckled arm, down to the fingers and back, imploringly, up the arm. It was the first time that they sat together beside the lake near the top of the town, and in his weekly letters he would often remind her of this thrilling encounter. His fingertips grew as moist as lips, but he did not dare to bring his head closer to hers. His hand retraced the confident route of the first caress, seeking to absorb her into himself. Speaking in a low voice, he quoted Gordon's words on bountiful nature and the cosmic experience that flows into the soul of man, while his hand continued to move slowly over the incredible plenitude of her arm. Then he dared to go further and told her about the decline of love in the big cities which had separated themselves from nature. Amid the surrounding spring (the earth stretching, catlike, after its winter's sleep, and one felt the deep breaths of the wheat and maize fields and of the vineyards which were budding and thickening their tendrils), Gordon was especially convincing and inspirational. Free Love? The prohibitions they had both brought from home were stronger than the new permissions (in later years, when she was a children's nurse and wanted to show how her pupils insulted each other with a raised middle finger, she did it by raising the ring finger—unable to overcome the home-bred inhibitions even as a demonstration). When they returned to town she introduced him to her parents, her face wearing the glow, the determination and commitment of a girl after her first night of love.

Now the hand which he put out to shake her father's hand was swollen and shaky. He licked the traces of the hospital's creamed vegetable soup from the corners of his mouth, and the picture which had evaded him rose before his mind's eyes. In his drowsy state, those caresses resembled the movements of chewing, yes, the remains of chewing movements, or else sucking at the breast. The strangeness of this thought was replaced a moment later by a twinge of longing and sorrow.

He awoke from his afternoon nap and inwardly complained about the superficial sleep, no thicker than the hospital sheet covering him. He missed those short, intense afternoon naps he used to catch during the long years when he was in charge of the kibbutz apple orchards. The sounds of clucking hens blended into his sleep, or the lowing of a calving cow. The nap was pleasantly warm, he could almost taste it, and would extend it by another minute, another five minutes—like self-indulgence with an extra piece of the Sabbath cake served at the festive Friday night suppers. His wife was still at his bedside, in the same bowed posture as before he had dozed off. For a moment he thought that it was Faigeh, his mother—who died aged sixty in his native town soon after he left for Eretz Israel—looking a good deal older, who was sitting beside his bed. The old gray sweater she was wearing made him feel at home in this room in which all the beds, sheets, and blankets bore the emblem of the hospital.

His wife smiled at him and her short fingers awoke and resumed stroking his hand. His heart was very weak, his kidneys were failing, and his poisoned body swelled like a shapeless plasticine doll. She hardly recognized the broad-shouldered man who had fallen in love with her sixty-one years before. Go, said her caress. Go, said the touch of her palm on the dry skin of his hand. Go, she urged him, like a mother encouraging her child to leave her apron strings and join the group of children walking to the first-grade classroom. Go on, said her hand—here now there's only suffering.

II

WORDS

Pampered Children—Nehemiah

A.

The word "devils" came later. First there were the darkness and its devils which cast their shadows on the walls. Screaming or crying did not persist long and curdled into dark shivers. The word "terror" came later.

In the beginning was the night. In the dark children's house Nehemiah did not dare to go alone to the toilet and woke up Avigdora. They went hand in hand, two white patches on the background of the black doorway, and hand in hand they returned to her bed. Then we heard Ronni's bare feet padding from room to room, till his sleepwalking led him to the entrance door and he vanished. It was night. Fear thickened the darkness and inserted thin devil hands between its particles. It was cold and shivery. Anxious sweat smelled like urine. Terror marked me to myself, the way a speeding pulse marks an injury. It was a slow night and there was no telling how much of it was left. The footsteps of Nehemiah and Avigdora walking to the bathroom and Ronni's somnabulic shuffling provided temporary security, as familiar, ordinary human activities can provide.

In the beginning was the fear. The children's house on the edge of the kibbutz was enveloped in darkness. Skinny devil arms moved unseen between the door and the bed and back. Whoever was sleeping slept, whoever was awake did not dare move a limb. Once in the night one heard the footsteps of the night watchman approaching from the nearby poultry coops. Whoever woke from a dream or thunder lay crying till the watchman's footsteps entered. Once Father was on night duty. Once a child jumped into his arms to shelter from the terror, and was carried to his parents. When they passed the lighted dining hall the smell of shame that came from Father was as tangible as the smell of sweat. What was said at home, what was done, that the child did not dare to ask for refuge there again? I can't remember a thing. Once I could not help myself and asked to go home, but never again. I lay in my bed and listened to the wailing of the jackals. It penetrated the darkened children's-house, piercing its walls. In the morning, Batya took us for a walk in the fields. Beyond our house stretched rows upon rows of cropped wheat fields, and Batya taught us the word "shelef"—stubble. Some saw stubble, others saw close rows of dusty, bristling jackal fur.

In the days leading up to the Suez War of 1956 infiltrators from the nearby Jordanian border broke in and blew up a flat and an electric pole. The members dug defensive trenches near the houses, exchanged views, advice, and fears. The talkers talked twice as much, the silent ones were twice as silent. Powerful lights were installed along the kibbutz fence, and we slept two to a bed in the shelter near the children's house. Now there were solid reasons to fear the night. When these were gone, only the jackals' wails and the night's loneliness remained, and these were easy to cope with. I'd lie awake and calm, recognizing the footsteps of the parents who arrived late and hearing them recede along the pavement. I came to know the body's slight warming before sleep, the quiet heaviness that began in the feet and rose slowly up the body till it swallowed me up. A discernible order began to emerge from the darkness, like the healing of a wound.

When that war ended we were big children, twelve years old, and after supper we'd play tag or rounders on the lawn in front of the dining hall, or spread through the kibbutz, playing night games with our counselors or without. And in summer the light did not end at all, because right after supper every class gathered around its own campfire in the field near the culture hall, and boiled sweet corncobs in big olive cans. The slope was all lit up, like a festive gypsy camp. It was warm around the campfires and between them. The heat melted the barriers between boys and girls and between us and the kids from the higher grades, all of us tanned by the dark, tanned by the flames. When parents pleaded with us to visit them in the evenings, we'd respond with a cocky grin that outsiders (visiting relatives, old friends from the parents' native towns, or a visiting American psychologist come to study the marvels of kibbutz upbringing) interpreted as a sign of mental health. Shrewder observers would have discerned that our cheeky grins were spread, like camouflage nets, over scorched, scarred skin. In two or three years we would begin to fall in love and other boys and girls would fall in love with us, and this love would expose our disability, because the thickened skin is quick to resist and to suspect, and caressing a scar means caressing too little and too late.

B.

In the beginning was the fear. Over it grew, like the misshapen bark on a sawn-off branch, expression of laughter, of bravery and arrogance.

Nehemiah knows that formal words of sympathy won't do for us, and he shakes my hand with a strained smile. He surveys the gathering in the room, standing near the door with his legs a little apart, the posture of a senior officer just lately out of uniform. The double curl of his fair hair has thinned and turned gray. Dinah urges him to sit down and have something to drink, but I have different plans for him. "What do you remember about our children's house?" I ask him when we settle down in my parents' bedroom. We haven't seen each other for years, and we've never talked about those nights. He glanced at me warily—a kibbutz habit of avoiding unnecessary self-exposure. "Forget it," he says. "Forget it." His father, who died years ago, was one of the silent members, those who did not speak up in the general meetings or through the kibbutz paper, who took care to be at work at six in the morning and returned home quietly as evening fell. I remember him well, standing at the taps in the dining hall entrance, scrubbing machine oil from his hands, looking in silence at people coming and going. Living next door to Ozer Huldai, the principal of the local school, who was always paying lip service to the kibbutz ideal of equality, only underscored the father's humble status. Now, to my surprise, Nehemiah tells me that his father urged him to leave the kibbutz from an early age. He tells me about his new family and the house he has recently bought, and we exchange phone numbers.

"You see," he says, sitting down again, "I don't know how you went through it. I had terrible fears, so I worked out a routine: I had to go to the toilet but I was scared to go alone. So I'd wake Avigdora and when we returned I'd get into her bed. So I'd start the night in my bed and wake up in the morning in hers. But didn't Ronni and Batsheva walk among the beds in their sleep?" he adds by way of justification. And then, with the awkward grin I recall from our childhood, he says, "I'm no psychologist, but if you ask me, my whole military career was an attempt to stay in my own bed through the night." He got up to leave. "Forget it," he says. "Just forget it."

A Decent Society

"Tell them you'll be a bit late," I say to Nehemiah. "You're visiting the bereaved, it's OK."

"Remember?" he smiles to himself, "they used to put a plate with hard-boiled eggs on our table. You must know this—when you hit two eggs together only one breaks. You keep hitting, the broken one will go on breaking and the other one will remain whole. When I was little I used to think that both eggs should break, maybe not as much, but still both. I felt there was something unjust, something not fair about it."

"I thought you were one of the unbreaking eggs," I say cautiously, to avoid trespassing.

"Funny," he says, "when we rode in the cart I could hit the mule till the stick turned red. No problem. But the chickens we took to the kitchen went on jumping in my mind for months."

I stared at him in astonishment. He noticed, but did not react. "The first time I took the goats to pasture one of them caught an udder on the barbed-wire fence of the children's livestock pen. It left a streak of milk and blood. I remember the green grass, early winter grass, and the wet black earth, and the red and white drops that got smeared on it. For weeks this picture bothered me before falling asleep. I can still remember that goat's long udder, it was so hard to milk. Up until a few years ago I could even remember her name. Funny what we remember," he says quietly, "such little things." Again he grins apologetically, as if he's exposed more than he'd meant to do. How carefully we guarded ourselves within the walls of the children's house, how skilled we became at hiding our daytime

53

and nighttime distresses from each other. A headless chicken hopped at night between our beds, and I didn't know.

It was winter, the pavements were covered with mud, and my name was on the roster to help in the poultry yard together with Hayim Levy, an "outside child" who was a classmate of my brother Elan. "We've got to bring two chickens to the kitchen today," Hayim said when we met near the coops. He had just two pimples on his smooth clean face. A cold wind carried bits of straw and the moos of cows from the nearby cowshed. "If we have to," I replied in a grown-up tone and followed him into the coops. We scattered feed and filled the water troughs. The hens ran away from us, glancing in all directions with their heads raised, as if we'd interrupted their conversations. In one of the laying boxes I found a pliable, translucent egg. Its naked membrane crinkled in the hand like fine cloth. "You find such an egg every week or two." Hayim's dark eyes examined the egg in my hand. "Enough, throw it away." He flung it against the wall of the coop, grinning at me as if he'd found me out.

"Now help me to catch them," he said. We chased a few hens into a corner and approached them with our arms outstretched. They clambered over each other, crapping in alarm and trying to fly. I reached out and caught one of them. The chicken flapped its wings, and I clutched it in my arms. "Here, I'll show you," said Hayim; he took the wings of the bird he'd caught and crossed them. Its wings interlocked, the hen stood quietly, clucking softly to itself, as if it was feeling very tired. "What now?" I asked. Our green sweaters were covered with tiny round feathers. "What now?—Now we kill them," he snapped. All the excitement and pleasure disappeared at once, and I followed him on wooden legs.

Hayim stopped near a big eucalyptus beside the coops. "The hell with it!" he said, tugged his work pants up above the brown work boots and stepped on the chicken's head. He pulled it by the legs as hard as he could. The neck stretched and stretched, but did not tear. It became completely exposed, a bundle of tiny bones, blood, and white sinews. The wintry wind blew right through me as if I was hollow. He straightened up. "One's finished," he said and flung it down. Blood burst from the torn neck as from a pump, reddened the white feathers and soaked into the black soil. The hen jumped crazily in every direction, stood, stumbled, leaped up with its wings outspread, and fell down on its shattered head. It looked as if it would attack us in a minute. The twisted neck was on the ground, but the feet kept on marching, as if the bird was ready to give up flying but not walking. Finally the information reached the feet and they ceased paddling against the ground and stopped still. The bloodied body collapsed, one leg sticking up in the air, the other folded against its belly. I was sitting down, bent double like a broken branch. Alarmed, I thought that in another few years it would be my turn to show some younger kid how to cross a hen's wings.

"We finished early today. Come, let's go home," Hayim is speaking to me from a distance. On the ground lies a second chicken head. This one also has an open, crooked beak and a blue comb. Its right eye is staring upward, round and calm. We carry the buckets with the eggs in one hand and the chickens in the other. A bluish winter moon hangs overhead, following the pearls of blood we shed on the muddy road. Near the kibbutz office we encounter Shlomo, the treasurer, who flings at us as he passes, "Come on, then, boys!" his big Adam's apple bobbing up and down in his stringy neck.

"Next week's Hanukkah," Hayim Levy informs me when we leave the dining hall. His hair is neatly combed, as if he's just come out of the barber shop. "Maybe my Father'll come and take me home." His plans don't interest me. A hen with a twisted neck keeps hopping madly inside my head, noisily flapping its reddened wings. In a couple of years I shall have my bar mitzvah. Afterwards I shall also have to separate hens from their heads. We're a decent society. I'm given two years to build up a flock of slaughtered chickens in my mind. In two years I'll also be capable of asking Igloo how're things with a well-aimed blow at his head. The fist clutching my lungs begins to loosen its grip. All at once the future looks less scary, more comprehensible.

Words

A.

Now and then, on my daily walks to the row of children's houses (once through the gloomy dining hall and the nearby water tower, of which only the concrete shell remains, and once via the laundry and the nearby air-raid shelter, to which Father carried me one night, in a wet pajama, before the kibbutz was evacuated as the battle front drew near), I recollect moments that preceded the words. I experience a dim sensation, remnant of those days: the words are not on my side.

Words appeared uninvited in the children's house. We were sitting on a mound of dirt not far from the shelter near the children's house, and Batya suggested that we race each other to the shelter. The word "race" rustled strangely in my head, like the taste of blood in the mouth, either because of its sound or Batya's tense expression. I remember the feel of the dry grass on my bare soles as I hurried downhill to the shelter, but chiefly I remember being surprised that I'd understood at once what I had to do, though I'd never before heard the word "race." Something about the body's motion as I ran, perhaps the exaggerated roll of the pelvis, or the body's swinging from side to side as I struggled for balance, tells me that I was not more than two. Batya ran faster and urged the last children to reach the shelter. I was glad to be one of the first to get there. There was a hidden menace in the new word, and Batya's tense smile did not dispel it. (Already this memory, like an ancient parchment exposed to the light, is beginning to fade, and in a moment I shall have difficulty distinguishing the actual memory from this telling of it.)

Other words opened menacing gaps in the world. "My bosom hurts,"

Mom complained when she finished breast-feeding Dinah. "Bosom? What's a bosom?" Mom pointed to her big bust, already covered by her clothes and the white apron of a children's nurse that she always wore. One evening afterwards, when we were chatting, as usual, from bed to bed after lights out, Batsheva asked did anyone know the name of the bulging part of women's bodies. I said, "Bosom." "No, it's called breasts," Batsheva asserted. The word "breasts" burst in my face, demolished the soft, protected mound above Mom's belly, and exposed underneath two frightening red lumps of flesh.

War was coming, and soldiers would drive by the kibbutz in jeeps on their way to the woods, looking for a water faucet or a patch of shade. Words and shreds of conversation wafted to the dining hall and the children's houses. Glasses of water awaited us in the kindergarten when we returned sweaty from walking in the fields. Nehemiah quietly tried to persuade me to do as he did—to contain myself and not drink, so as to adapt ourselves ahead of time to the "water discipline." The words "water discipline" echoed in the room in solemn tones and expression, stood for a different world, a world of exhausting hikes and harsh self-control. Nehemiah's was the only way to dispel the fear: to become soldiers from now— small, secret recruits, aged four.

After the War of Independence, donkeys sometimes wandered over from the abandoned Arab villages around the kibbutz. One Saturday Elan suggested that we take a ride on a newly captured donkey. It was morning, and the kibbutz paths and gardens sprawled in the still heat which could make the senses drowse or suddenly stir you into getting up and doing things. The donkey looked at us with its moist brown dog's eyes and blew hard into the handful of alfalfa we threw down to it. We opened the warm iron gate of the shed and rode out. I enjoyed riding on the big donkey's warm, hay-smelling back, Elan holding the reins and me hugging him from behind. When we reached the hen coop near the kibbutz gate we ran into Gideon, who yelled at us to take the donkey back to the shed right away. Gideon was a secondary-school boy, so Elan did not argue. On the way back Elan said, "Gideon is a rotter." In my ears the new word was like the first bite on an apple which reveals its texture and taste. I knew immediately what it meant, as if it had always been in my head, and I only needed to hear it once to know how to use it.

Other words turned up in the children's house and spread through the rooms. In kindergarten we danced in a circle before lunch. Ronni crept up behind me and pulled my underpants down to my knees. Deeply offended, I threw him to the floor. He stood up looking pale, and there was a horrible depression in his forehead. Batya rushed him to the clinic and came back looking as pale as Ronni. She said quietly that Ronni had a brain concussion and would remain in bed at his parents' place for several days. The words "brain concussion" hung in the air, strange and terrifying, and I hoped they would not prevent the depression in Ronni's head from smoothing out. The next day Batya asked me if I was sorry for what I'd done, and if I had visited Ronni and asked how he was. Clearly there was something wrong with me—I'd never thought of doing any of it. That afternoon I went to his house, my head held between those new words like a cow's head between the bars of the trough.

What does memory remember? The friction of body against body, of flesh against a door, a crushed entry into words.

B.

Out of our new radio in the brown wooden box booms Ben Gurion's energetic voice. Father sits beside the window in shorts and vest, listening to the speech. "Listen, it's like good music," he says, inviting me to sit beside him, as though he'd gotten me a seat at a rare concert. I did not hear any music nor could I follow the words, only the tone, which rose every few words, as if the speaker was striking the table before him. Father and his comrades doted on words—Zionism, socialism, equality, cooperation, mutual help, volunteering, and crop rotation—the way people dote on pets. Every argument ended in a quarrel, because someone had insulted their words. I also loved words, but in a different way. In the book *Winnetu and the Shatterhand,* it said that Winnetu filled the white man with dread, and the word "dread" sent a pleasant shiver through me. I saw in my mind's eye Winnetu rising on his brown horse, his ribs outlined on his bare chest like long feathers, his steady warm eyes gazing fearlessly at the green valley below. Similarly, in Bible lessons we learned about Abraham's servant who went forth to find a wife for Isaac, and saw beside the well a "damsel" who was "very fair to look upon." In the text the word *na'arah*—damsel—lacks the final letter, so that it looks like *na'ar*—lad—and this thrilled me. It was as though a stone had broken and I could look into its core, could see what it had been before it solidified. The missing letter made me happy—I'd always known that the two were really one.

Mom returned from work and sat down heavily in the chair on the porch to take off her shoes. "Do you love me?" Dinah raised Mom's chin to make her look at her. Mom gave her a tired smile. "Do you love me?" Dinah persisted. Mom asked me to play with Dinah a little, so I took her to see the chicks Elan and I were raising under the house. I could hear the voices of children playing on the big lawn in front of the dining hall. "I'm going to play," I told Mom. "What about Dinah?" "She's almost five. She can amuse herself for a bit." Dinah's eyes looked at me reproachfully over her bulging red baby's cheeks.

Elan and his classmates were playing tag on the big lawn. This was my best game—even bigger boys had a hard time catching up with me. The sun was going down behind the culture hall, and on the lawn the sunset blended with the clear light from the dining hall windows and the greenish evening glow of the grass. A soft breeze carried faint sounds of sheep and cows. Even Ben Gurion's voice sounded softer by the time it reached this place. The game was finished, some of the bigger kids were going home, and it seemed it wouldn't start again. Shmuel and Yitzhak, Elan's classmates, talked quietly on the side and then came up to me. "Wanna bet I can beat you running to the edge of the lawn?" asked Shmuel. "What shall we bet on?" "A slap in the face," his fox's face grinned. "Go on, bet him!" other kids urged me. I tried to catch Elan's eyes, but saw only his powerful, broad back. Elan wasn't as fast as I, but he was the strongest boy in his class.

Yitzhak drew a line on the ground beyond the north edge of the lawn and said he would "starter" us. Yitzhak and Shmuel had already had their bar mitzvah, and I was pleased that they were talking to me as to an equal. I didn't know the term "starter" but understood the idea and nodded. The boys went over to the finishing line, and Shmuel and I crouched in readiness. "Ready steady go," Yitzhak shouted quickly. I assumed that this was the starter and began to run, but Shmuel was already far from the starting line, and all I could see in the dusk was his green shirt which looked black. Usually when running a race I felt, after a few dozen meters, that the ground was pushing me forward the way a wave carries a swimmer to the shore. But the grass was short and did not carry me forward, and Shmuel crossed the finishing line before me.

Shmuel went away to prepare the slap in the face, and my classmates hurried home. I refrained from asking what was the difference between a slap in the face and a smack, or what there was to prepare. Yitzhak glanced at me and then joined Shmuel, and Ronni quietly tried to persuade me to call off the bet, because it was known that Shmuel was a rotter. This fitted neatly in my mind with the fact that he was a neighbor and friend of Gideon's. "Maybe he's a rotter, but I gave my word," I said, as though "a slap in the face" were words I had yet to learn. In the darkness the first stars came out, and we heard Ronni's mother calling him from afar. "Well, I'm going home," Elan announced. "I'll be along in a little while," I said, trying to sound as if I had some business to conclude. His strong, massive body—Father's body—vanished in the darkness. The awareness that I was alone in the world struck me like a blow. The lighted squares of the dining hall windows were some distance away, and Ben Gurion's voice could still be heard, stopping with a thump every few words.

I sat down on the grass, clasping my bare knees, crouched like a rabbit that is trying to be bold and fearless: its body always sways a little when it breathes, and now every inhalation broke down into many tiny shivers. "I'm ready," announced Shmuel, coming up, his right hand raised, covered with a layer of black mud. His eyes gleamed as he looked at Yitzhak. Yitzhak went behind me and pressed my arms to my back. Like a boy trying to prove himself to his older buddies, I understood that this was part of the bet. The people on duty in the dining hall were hurrying from table to table, putting down bowls of vegetables and bread. Shmuel touched my face with his left hand, half patting my jaw, half gripping it, and already I knew that it had been a joke, and that having shown that I kept my word, I was free to go home at last.

That is a slap in the face, and Shmuel is a rotter, I repeated to myself on the way home. That is a slap in the face, and Shmuel is a rotter. The words helped to calm the shiver that rose from my stomach. Elan saw me from the porch and quickly led me to the faucet beside the house. I lowered my face to the current and he washed it carefully and quickly. We didn't exchange a word or a look, because we both understood that there were some things you didn't talk about, and there was no point in getting mad at him, because he didn't make the rules, and in the kibbutz your classmates are your family, and I was silly to think otherwise. Or I could get mad at him but it would be a pity, because I didn't have too many friends and the kibbutz was full of rotters, so I should be more careful next time.

In the meantime Ben Gurion finished speaking and Father had left for the dining hall. "What happened to your face?" Mum asked. Elan went to his desk to do his homework. "We were playing and I fell on the grass." My voice came from the back of the throat, thick and harsh, suppressing the pleading tone that might reveal how vulnerable the skin was, how badly I needed a hand to melt the remaining tremor. Mom was teaching the alphabet to Dinah, who was about to go to bed. I pressed my finger to her red cheek and it left a white mark. Thinking about all the words she still had to learn, I gave her a tight hug. She smiled happily and clasped my head with her rosy hands. I closed my eyes between her short arms. A wave of warmth I had no words for rose from my chest to my throat. "Kiss," she said, giving me her cheek which had regained its color. "Kiss!"

A Lost War

A.

Wednesday, the second night of the shivah. Raheli and I are about to retire to the apartment the kibbutz has lent us, but a knock on the door stops us at the table. Batya, my first kindergarten teacher, enters, apologetic—she saw the light and decided to come in despite the late hour.

On my daily walk today I went into the dining hall. There was nothing left of the old lunchtime hubbub. Here and there sat solitary survivors of my parents' generation. Sarah, the mother of my classmate Yossi, was balancing her tray on her zimmer frame as she advanced toward a table. When she saw me she smiled, then mumbled awkwardly, "What we've come to," and shuffled on. Her embarrassed words expressed sorrow: my husband too died this year, and you must remember us, how we used to walk briskly to the cowshed and the orchard and the children's house. Who would have thought that one day we'd drag ourselves with difficulty from the house to the dining hall. And there was also a complaint: who would have thought that one's body would shrivel to the size of a child's body, that we would sit by ourselves in the dining hall like scolded children, or that loneliness would hurt more, day and night, than the aching joints of the fragile, chilly body.

Batya hugs Mom, and their sad smiles speak of resignation and complaint: what we've come to.

Despite her age, Batya's walk is still firm, her hair is thick and groomed, and her smile still has something of the brightness I recall from childhood. Mom never tires of talking about Father's last days and hours, and Batya naturally plays her part in the ritual. "Yonah had a terrible old age," Mom sighs. "I never imagined that that's what would happen. Never imagined . . ." Batya asks questions and Mom answers, and I, sitting in the corner nearby, go back almost half a century—a four-year-old seeing the aging of things in the toy cupboard and realizing, with a stab of anxiety, that nothing can escape it.

B.

Batya gave each of us a grapefruit half for our midmorning snack. We were sitting in a circle under the eucalyptus tree behind the children's house, not far from the air-raid shelter where we slept at night. Green sunbeams warmed the dry eucalyptus leaves on the black earth, making them pleasant to walk on with bare feet. Batya brought tin knives from the games corner and suggested that we make shapes out of the grapefruit shells. No problem. I carved two holes for the eyes, a triangular nose, and a mouth. Very carefully I cut two rows of big teeth in the mouth. The mask began to smile even before I finished. It filled me with happy power.

In the evening I put the mask in the little wooden cabinet in which Elan and I kept our things. We already had a set of checkers and a few spent cartridges. Now for some days I also have a happy mask in there.

After supper I run home to look at my mask. Elan is not yet back from school, and Mom will come in later. A shocking sour smell greets me when I open the cabinet door. White circles have spread over the mask and wrinkled it. Blue flowers of decay cluster around the frozen eyes. Brown stains cover the sunken cheeks. The smile has collapsed like an old man's mouth, rimmed with white sugar. I stand petrified in front of the dead mask, feeling a huge hole gaping in my chest, as if I've been shot. My trembling heart knows that nothing will ever be the same again.

I sit on the porch to wait for Mom. Bananas rot in an ugly way, a sweet smell softens and darkens them. A lemon does not turn dark. Its skin gradually yellows, then turns brown like the coins we put into the JNF box on Sabbath eve. In the corner of the children's house stands a straw basket with pomegranates, by way of decoration, and a lemon is hiding among them. It's brown and dry on the outside, warm and wet inside, and it lies curled up like a sleeping baby. Someone's coming down the path. I strain to see if it's Mom, but it isn't. I shut my eyes and try again, but it's still only our neighbor who works in the dairy. His daughter is in kindergarten with me, but he doesn't have a wife. He had a wife once, but she's not there any more. The wife's face appears before me like a scary mask, then vanishes.

"Why are you looking at me like this?" Mom asks when she arrives. There are red cobwebs in her eyes, and the freckles on her face have grown in the heat. Only now I discover that her forehead is divided across its width into several smaller foreheads.

It's dark outside when Mom takes me to the children's house. Because of the blackout the kibbutz is in total darkness, and the houses sway with the trees. Just when we pass near the laundry we hear short buzzes that pass overhead at great speed and disappear in the darkness. Some of them hit the high water tower near the dining hall, strike off noisy sparks, fizz briefly on the concrete wall and fall silent. "My faigaleh," Mom says, as if something has happened to me. Bent double, we run through the darkness that tangles thickly around our legs, though I don't know why we're running. Mom opens the door of the air-raid shelter and quickly shuts it behind us. Her face stiff, she takes me to the bathroom and helps me to brush my teeth. She covers me and sits beside me. In the dim light in the shelter her face is a pallid mask. "My faigaleh." She tries to close my eyes, which keep staring at her. "It'll be all right, you'll see, everything will be all right." She strokes my hair, unaware that I already know what will happen in a week or two to the holes which are her eyes and her smile.

A Wet Icicle

A.

"Frankly, he worried me. Other children looked for love in each other, but he looked for it in me," Batya tells Mom. I'm sitting near the sink, once again a child who can be discussed in his presence. "On the other hand, he argued with me the way no other child did. He talked to me like a grown-up, angrily, as if he was giving up on me. A strange mixture of weakness and strength that I never understood."

"You called her Bootie, remember?" Mom turns to me with a faint smile. Batya and I smile at each other (a little overenthusiastically, trying to cheer Mom up, as though bereavement has turned her into a child). I gladly confirm the name "Bootie," though in fact I remember it only from Mom's stories. Throughout my earliest years Batya woke us up in the morning, set the tables and gave us our food, swept and washed the floors of the children's house, turned off the lights at night, and wished us a good night before leaving. One day she took over another group and we got a new nurse. Did I miss her when she left? I probably did, though I don't remember it. I spent all my early years in her presence, yet I never think of her except when I visit the kibbutz, when we happen to pass each other and exchange friendly smiles. During those years I saw Mom only at the end of the day, mostly at bedtime. Before leaving me, Mom would squeeze my hand, compressing all her caresses into one. This is the immemorial parting gesture of those who must leave too soon. How did I call out to her in those years? From under the blanket, soundlessly, with my whole curled up body.

B.

The long, rounded popsicle, of which each of us got a half, was a surprise. Not only the chill compressed into the dripping candy, not just the white sweetness which never disappointed the tongue till it had all melted away between the lips, but the fact that it was a chunk of sheer delight, not a food that must be eaten up and never left on the plate at any time, let alone in wartime. I remember a beach, waves of people, a road sunning itself like a lizard in the sand, and this surprise: a wet sweetness designed only to give pleasure.

One morning, a few days earlier, we were awakened early and loaded on buses. Later we would learn that an emergency meeting had led to the decision to evacuate the children because of the advancing Iraqi army, which had already fired on the kibbutz walls. I planted my feet before the high stairs of the bus, in which my big brother was already seated, and refused to budge. Strong hands picked me up and put me on the other bus. I didn't ask about Mom that morning. Mom was busy. Mom was a children's nurse.

Mom was a nurse in Tel Aviv, too. Only more tired than in the kibbutz, her freckled face red from the heat. I'm in Kindergarten One, and Mom is the nurse of Kindergarten Two. During the day I see her walking with her children to and from the beach, their white clothes take their color from her eternal white apron. The apron recedes from me like a sail, and I'm careful not to cross the invisible boundary between us. When I was small I tried to pull the apron off her. "Take it off and be Saturday," I begged. Now I'm a big boy and can understand what I'm being told. I must stay dry.

After lunch Mom crosses the lawn in Meir Park, the children following her like a row of chicks. The children in my kindergarten are playing tag, and I play tag with her. Turn around, turn around now, I tell her in a low voice. The sea breeze carries the words to other ears, and other women suddenly turn around and wave, or grab their hats. Mom walks away, sits down on a bench at the far end, wipes her face with a handkerchief. I'm clutching a brown shoelace in my sweaty hand.

Mom had made a game out of two shoelaces: I hold the string taut between my hands, and she takes it from me and quickly turns it into all kinds of triangles and rectangles. By working very carefully I manage to transfer the complicated structure to my own hands. She had contrived to turn the string into a carpet design and a hammock, then I take it all apart. That's our game. There are no other toys, but there will be no shortage of torn shoelaces, because Mom is a nurse. It's our game, and we play it very seriously, without giggling or hugging, only a pat on the head, to smooth the hair. But I know how to make embraces: when I lean against her wide body, she surrounds me with her arms.

Not all the children have a mother in Tel Aviv to put them to bed. There's no room for a chair between the beds, so Mom sits on my bed, hands on knees, and sings about the winter cyclamen, about shepherds, and toys going to sleep. She sings softly, confining the songs to my bed, as when you water a tree and make sure the water does not run out of its bed. There's a sharp, stiff piece of iron in my chest, and I can't fall asleep till it softens. "All the toys have gone to sleep—teddy, ball and spinning-top, lully, lully lull," the last words sound a pleading note that alarms me—in a moment she'll get up and leave. Mom has been on her feet all day, and tomorrow she has to get up early, and I must be a good boy. "Now a song about a bird," I beg, and then, "about a tree." I know I'm crossing the line, but fear is stronger than shame, and it's already established that I'm a bad boy who doesn't listen.

The classroom in which we are housed is quite dark. "Now a song about a chair," I beg, but Mom is tired. She tries to regain control by singing the familiar songs: "Still and calm lies the village, lo the flocks are coming home." Instead of carrying me back to the kibbutz flocks, returning at sundown from the direction of the stony hill, her voice brings me closer to her broad body. Beside my head is this big body in a white apron, sheltering me as the rock shelters the cyclamen, but the body has wishes of its own, and right now it wishes to leave me. If earlier I felt a certain tiredness, now I'm wide awake. The piece of iron, which had turned into a noodle, is once again stiff and sharp. But Mom withdraws her arm, takes my hand in her warm palm, and gives it a quick squeeze to sweeten the parting. Then her good-bye turns into a kiss on the forehead and her receding back. At the far end of the room her body is a thicker part of the darkness, and now I can only hear her slow footsteps in the silent school-house. I make an effort to hear those footsteps longer, until she reaches her room, her bed. For a moment I succeed, but soon the sound is lost, and I can't distinguish it from the medley of noises from the street. I'm alone in the alien darkness.

As soon as Mom's footsteps vanish I switch to a defensive posture, lie on my side, facing the middle of the room, my legs folded against my stomach. I don't need to go to the toilet yet, but I'm memorizing the route to it. The crying of jackals doesn't reach this place, and the strange room is less scary than I'd thought. I loosen up and take a chance on turning to the wall. But I soon turn back to the room, knowing I shouldn't have faced the wall. A white figure is passing among the beds, disappears into the corridor, and reappears in our room, walking among the crowded beds without bumping into them. Mom, I want to yell, Mom, but I don't even know where she is sleeping. I shut my eyes. Nothing. I saw nothing.

I know I've been sleeping, because now I've woken up. Occasionally, after I've slept for a few hours, I find a break, like an air bubble in a drinking straw. I like to lie in this break with my eyes shut, watching a huge red ball which moves away and falls apart into a lot of yellow balls, and these turn into shoals of blue, black, and red goldfish. Sometimes the yellow turns into a warm fur, a kangaroo's moist pouch, or a brown sun going down over the beach and becoming a vast field of sand, and sometimes it fades away and I can feel the touch of Mom's white apron in my hands. When I open my eyes in the children's house and see the chair and my clothes beside the bed, the break closes up. Tonight there is no break. Fear passed through the sleep like a wave passing through the people swimming back to the beach.

When I get back from the toilet the bed is cold and scratchy. I shut my eyes and find, happily, that a little corner of sleep remains on the side of my head. I try to squeeze myself into it, but my legs remain outside, and they slowly drag off the blanket of sleep. Morning arrives. A gray light rises from the roads and sidewalks and slowly fills the room. When at last the nurse comes in, she says that it happens, but I must try not to let it happen again. Her irritation shows in the sharp movements with which she strips the sheet from the bed. I can't tell her that I'm really trying and that I know I should stay dry, because it's hard to talk to someone who's changing your wet sheet. I get dressed, go out, and mix with the other kids in the paved courtyard.

The long wet popsicle that each of us got a half of was a surprise. This white roll is neither solid nor liquid, or perhaps both. How do we eat it, we ask Batya, giggling with pleasure, showing each other different tricks, seeing what licking, sucking, and biting can do to the cold chunk of delight. Life can be pleasant and hold surprises and good things, even here on Tel Aviv's beach. From afar I see Mom's whitish form, surrounded by her kids, moving away from me like a sail. I close my eyes and suck the white popsicle, drinking in its motherly sweetness.

What Memory Recalls

Alarm and fear, memory's diligent trainers. Under their supervision, memory will do the same exercise day after day, nor will they let up at night, ensuring that it reaches middle age safely: I'm standing all soaped up in a strange shower, the weekly shower to which we are taken from the schoolhouse where we're staying in Tel Aviv. The nurses assure us that as soon as the war ends we'll go back to the kibbutz, but already we've been in Tel Aviv for several long weeks. Suddenly the air-raid siren sounds, wails rising and falling, like the cries of the jackals at night, and the building shakes and groans. In time to come, I'd learn that the Egyptian air force was attacking Tel Aviv, but as a child I have no idea what is happening, I only know it's scary, awfully scary. The corridor is full of bits of plaster and glass. Fear gushes in me like blood, and the floor is slippery under my wet feet so I can't run. Surprisingly, the walls remain standing, and I can lean against them, breathing hard, while through my mind flickers a complaint against a world that doesn't let a four-year-old boy finish his weekly shower in peace. Then the sky goes quiet and the house calms down, and then another siren sounds, stretched along the streets at the level of the electric lines, falls silent and takes away the memory. Where did I run, soapy all over? When did I see Mom again? Freed of its trainers, memory grew lazy and slack, and lost it.

Similarly, I can't find even a shred of memory from the return home and the renewed familiarity with the children's house. Memory preserved the fall, not the rising up again. Only the announcement made by Esther, the nurse, that from now on we need not stay close to the air-raid shelter suggests that the child emerging from the shelter—well aware of the solemnity of the occasion, but not its cause—has returned from Tel Aviv.

Likewise, the envy he feels for the colorful hens installed in the small enclosure behind the children's house shows that we're back from Tel Aviv. The reddish-brown chickens flap their wings noisily when they come out of the two wire cages, rush forward with lowered heads, slow down, and start pecking the orangey sorghum seeds we scatter for them on the ground. I can recall the astonishment and the envy: they've only just been caught, caged, and brought over to us, and already they're pecking at the ground and raking the eucalyptus leaves as if this has always been their home. Surprise and envy are also among memory's diligent trainers.

The surprise. When we were in kindergarten we were taken on a kibbutz truck to Luna Park in Tel Aviv, and the whole way there we sang "Four on the speeding jeep," "Samson's foxes," and "Always first on the line." In the middle of the loud singing I saw the nurse Yaffah mouthing to the woman beside her: "Look at him!" For a moment I saw myself from outside: a skinny, freckled boy, his singing throat outstretched in complete self-oblivion. I caught this glimpse of him as in a mirror, a second before the mirror caught him for all time. A spasm of surprise passed over his face, like the spasm that passes through a branch when it is thrown on the fire.

And the envy. When we started secondary school we moved into a children's house that did not have a dining room, so throughout those years we ate in the kibbutz dining hall. Three times a day I'd walk through the revolving glass doors, chat with other kids on my way to a table, laugh, casually smooth down my hair. Every gesture was reflected in the faces of the members seated there as in dozens of mirrors. Together with Lusha the nurse, Ze'ev the teacher, and the other kids, I'd watch him from the side and he looked back at me, self-conscious, and all the while something cracked, dwindled, lost its suppleness, grew stiff, as though I'd become "the man in the wall," a wall in the hall of mirrors. In the afternoon I'd walk with Dinah to the cowshed and the sheep pen. She'd press her forehead to the dusty fence of the sheepfold and watch the lambs, mesmerized. Now and then I'd enter the compound, which was covered with turds, catch one of the lambs, and hold it up for her to pet—always amazed that its coat, which looked so soft, was in fact as coarse as a doormat. The lamb would wriggle in her hands, escape, and a moment later leap about in the compound, dash back and forth, butting imaginary foes. Dinah and I were merely a picture that penetrated its thick pelt for a moment and vanished. I always felt a twinge of envy.

What does memory recall? Whatever made its fine network vibrate, shook its filaments and creased it, opened a temporary crack which let in unexpected darkness, terror—or a brilliant light, the gleam of a sudden caress. The distortion slowed the flowing current, thickened the quick connections. The thickening captured forever the moments of darkness, the creases of light.

Most amazing are the body's lost memories. The first night after my arrival, before going to bed, my wife smoothed moisture lotion on my face, which felt dry after the long hours on planes. I shut my eyes and she passed her hand deftly on my face, as if it were a single surface, the nose and eyes insignificant obstacles. Her touch awakened a dim memory of a big, firm hand moving over my face (wiping my nose? applying protective cream against the sun?), and a wave of deep-seated warmth rose from the depths of my childhood. My face recalled only the hand, not the body behind it. Mom's hand? I doubt it. Something about its brisk motion tells me it was one of the nurses. The warmth it evoked suggests the pleasure it gave me. It handled me somewhat roughly, inconsiderately, but the passivity it imposed on me felt nice. Someone was taking care of me and I didn't have to do anything, only close my eyes.

Blue Bruises on the Flesh

Openings on Life

A.

Thursday. A knock on the door and Mom's old friend Hannah comes in with her son Aryeh. The wrinkled, stained brown winter coat hanging from her bowed shoulders betrays a neglected old age. Dinah invites her to join us for lunch, and Hannah sits down silently on the chair I pull out for her. She has brought no words of comfort, only her presence. Aryeh's eyes glance over me quickly. His firm stomach, that I recall too well, has grown into a middle-aged paunch. He sits on the corner of the sofa and doesn't taste a thing. His eyes are fixed on the blank television screen opposite. Dinah smiles at me in wonder. She asks Aryeh about his wife and children, and he replies vaguely. "And where is our dreaming brother now?" she says to me. I'm settling accounts with A. D. Gordon. His ideas about nature as a harmonious, benevolent deity, to which we must draw near and whose laws we must learn, strike me more than ever as quite baseless.

B.

The children's livestock farm, not far from our children's house, is a source of endless marvels. "When is Purim?" we yell the traditional cry at the turkeys in their compound, and they answer with a volley of loud gobbles. They've only been here a few weeks and already they're walking about ponderously, pecking pedantically at the ground, as though they've been

here since time immemorial. Crossing the compound, the big male
spreads his tail into a colorful fan. His wing feathers sweep the warm
earth, and his comb droops over his beak like solid drops of blood.
Thrusting out his breast, he circles the nearby hen, seizes her neck with
his beak, and makes her sit under him. He shifts his weight from leg to leg
till he's sitting comfortably, then slowly gets off her. The hen rises and
shakes her wings vigorously. In the adjoining compound the geese rush to
the corner, waddling like hurrying matrons. Not far from there the goats
are chewing hay with crooked jaws, and the billy goat peers at me with his
sly beard. This week we received a new batch of chicks, a swarm of little
ones who rush together from corner to corner, so yellow, as though
they've only this minute emerged from the yolk. You can watch them for
hours on end.

"Only the big children can work in the livestock farm," the teacher
Henya says to me. "There they learn personal responsibility." She delivers
the words "personal responsibility" carefully into my hands, so I wouldn't
drop them. The last rays of the sun are lying across the washed dining
room tables. Supper is over, and all the children have gone to their parents. "Go home, I'll finish up here," Henya says to Batya the nurse. "No,
no, I'll finish," Batya protests, offended.

"You're only in second grade, you'll have plenty of time to work when
you're older," says Mom. She's just come home from work, her face is
flushed, and she sits down to untie her shoelaces. I thought she'd be
pleased that I want to work in the children's livestock farm. "Do you have
a cold?" she asks. In the morning Batya cut a square out of an old bedsheet
for me to use as a handkerchief. I must have left it behind, on my desk in
the classroom, or perhaps on the bed. I've nothing to wipe my nose on,
and I try to shift the irritation from my nose to my throat. The sneeze
turns into a strangled cough. My three-year-old sister toddles towards me
on her plump little rubber feet. The inside of her left foot shows a tangle
of delicate blood vessels, as though that was where she was finished.
"Kiss," she says, offering me her face. "Can you take her for a little walk?"
Mom asks.

Before the afternoon rest I run out to look at the chicks. Aryeh is dish-
ing out their feed with a rectangular tin shovel. His wide jawbone juts out
like the stock of a hammer. Under his arm there is already a mass of brown
hairs that he likes to twirl around his finger. I lean on the fence, watching
the chicks running to the feed on hundreds of tiny legs, straight as match-

sticks. I ask if I can help. He measures me with his eyes and says, "We'll see, depends if you can be trusted." His jaw muscles continue to chew after he finishes speaking.

After lunch I hurry to the children's livestock farm. By now the chicks have turned white, and they no longer dash from place to place. One chick cheeps quietly to itself, like a child walking alone and talking to himself, another one spreads its wings and keeps raking the ground. The tail of a chick standing near the wire fence is red from pecking. It's a hot day, and green flies buzz through the air, glittering like splinters of glass. "We're getting a new batch of chicks this evening," Aryeh says to me. "If you come you could help us." He shifts his weight from foot to foot, a furrow of red sweat on his forehead. Will I be here? Of course I'll be here. Happiness patters inside me on hundreds of yellow matchstick legs.

Excited by the new responsibility, I wolf down my supper and rush outside. Darkness flows up from the fields over the dirt road leading to the poultry yard, like the tide over the beach. On the edge of the light from the children's house I stop a moment, take a deep breath, and run on. There is a different solidity in the earth, and the familiar coops seem to sway like trees in the wind. I slow down and advance cautiously in the strange air, surprised to discover night eyes in my head. There's a darkness child in me which has just woken up.

There is no one among the coops. The geese are sitting quietly on the ground; one of them breaks out in agitated quacking, rushes with a flapping of wings after its voice, and falls silent. Beside the hay shed I find Aryeh leaning against a post. "The batch didn't come today. Probably next week. But since you're here, come, sit down, we'll talk." He points to a stack of feed sacks inside the dark shed. A light wind is blowing and the hollow iron posts of the shed wail like jackals. I whistle a little and stop. The smell of the feed is tickling my nose, but I turn the sneeze into a cough.

"I'm glad you're taking such an interest in the chicks," Aryeh said quietly. "Shame there aren't more kids like you. Maybe from tomorrow we'll let you feed them yourself." I say nothing, only look down, almost bursting with joy. "Take you pants off a minute, I want to see what kind of underpants they give you," he says, twitching uneasily on the sacks. He grabs my shoulders with his strong hands, turns me around, and lays me on my stomach. In the same movement, as if in fun and only for a moment, he lies on top of me. There's no end to the delightful surprises today! A body is covering mine, the way I like, my whole body's being hugged, the way I like. But the sack is rough and something hard is shoving at my back forcefully. Alarm fills me, catching my breath, thumping wildly. He gets off me and makes me sit beside him. My slack body struggles to keep upright. For a moment we sit side by side in silence, hands on knees. I avoid looking at his gaping pants. From afar the lights of the children's houses look like blue bruises.

"Take off your underpants a minute," he says. "I want to see how they teach you to put them on." Amid the fear I hear his thoughts churning, hear him grinning sheepishly to himself, knowing that I know it's a lousy excuse. My boneless hands refuse to move. We hear voices approaching. Aryeh jumps up and hides behind the sacks. Some members are coming close. They walk among the coops and stop not far from us. "We should put a short piece about it in the circular," says the school principal. He speaks at dictation speed, and I know exactly how his thin lips meet over his big, tobacco-stained teeth. "But this is just the start," the teacher Henya presumes to intervene. "Next week we'll be getting laying hens and geese." The wind snatches the grown-ups' voices and I can't make out any more. With my whole body I hear Aryeh breathing beside me, feel his eyes sharp and hard, still unsure if I can be trusted. He pulls up his pants and indicates that I should do the same. When the grown-ups walk away toward the children's houses, we emerge from the obscurity of the shed. "Will I be allowed to feed the new chicks by myself?" I hear myself asking. "That doesn't count," the words barely escape from his powerful jaws.

All night the same scary dream. I'm on the beach and a huge wave, high as the cliff behind me, rises up toward me. I run to the staircase but stumble on the sand. Glancing back, I see that hundreds of chicks are riding on the foamy crest, as though they were ducklings. I get up and go to the bathroom. Before returning to the bedroom I sit for a few minutes in the dining room. The tables are already laid for breakfast. I know by heart where every one of us sits, and for a moment the dining room is filled with the rumpus of our mealtimes. But nothing helps. The dream hides with me under the blanket. Like a worn screw turning on its axis, I find myself again on the beach with the huge wave rising toward me. I run on the deep sand, fall into a hole some kid had dug, and wake up with a thump. When I fall asleep again, Aryeh is floating on the green sea on his flatboat, with chicks sitting on it like birds on a wire. I shout to him: "What do you mean, that doesn't count? What does count?" The prow of his flatboat almost cuts me in two when he passes behind me.

—Faigaleh mine, are you depressed or something?
—I'm not depressed.
—What are you then?
—Nothing, I'm nothing.
—Are you worried about something?
—I told you, I'm nothing.
—So what is it?
—Nothing, honestly.
—Shall I give you a piece of cake?
—Maybe later. Now I'm going to feed the chicks.
—But don't be long. It's Saturday, and I like our family to have at least our tea together.
—All right.

Because, though I'm only in second grade, everyone knows I'm crazy about chicks and I can be relied on. And Aryeh doesn't say anything when I go in alone to the newly arrived chicks. I open the gate, get the feed and put it down for them, then fill their dishes with water, doing everything responsibly and seriously, like a person who has earned his wage honestly.

Pampered Children—Yossi

We were in kindergarten, standing beside the air-raid shelter, waiting for Batya, when suddenly I knew with dizzying clarity: now Yossi will turn and look toward the dining-hall—and he did turn. Now he will bend down to tie his shoelace and say, she's always late—and he did and he said. Now he will start to walk toward the children's house—I was frightened—and he started to walk. By the time we moved to our new children's house, halfway through primary school, the faces surrounding me were already sealed and opaque. Only some involuntary inward gestures remained, as against the major physical ones, crying, vomiting, laughing.

Thursday afternoon. Despite the early hour, the place is full of visitors. I'm sitting with my old classmate Yossi in a corner of the room, between the television on the bookcase and the wide window overlooking the path. His father passed away a year ago, and he is visiting the bereaved house while on his weekly visit to his mother. Like the rest of our class, he has not grown fat, only thicker, and his hair, which has turned quite white, is cut in a short Roman fringe on his forehead. His mother's illness and loneliness, and the company of mourning visitors, soften his customary ironic smile. ("Mom's always providing me with a parcel, you know. Two avocados, three bananas, eight olives. She spends half the time I'm here packing. She might as well, since we don't have anything to talk about. To keep her happy, I take the things and dump them in the first bin I see. They're really poor here, you know. Every time I come I fill her fridge with things, but still she makes these parcels for me.") Over the years he's developed a tolerant attitude toward his surroundings, and this apparent maturity serves him as a barricade: "So Shlomo's getting divorced, right, what can

I do about it? She's crying? Well, so would I if I was being dumped. So what?" Dinah offers him coffee, but it turns out he's trying to cut down on coffee because of his stomach ulcer. Ulcer? Since when does he have an ulcer? There will be no shortage of subjects for conversation, then, with Batsheva, Shlomo, and Smadar, who promised to come this evening (Gastro? Zantac? A hot-water bottle?). The kibbutz educators did all they could to keep our parents away from us, but the overstretched nerves, the ulcers, and asthma stuck to the family inheritance without fail. "Remember what this place was like?" I ask rhetorically. "Suppertime the dining hall was packed, sometimes you had to wait for the table. There were heaps of youngsters sprawled on the big lawn, and the whole kibbutz was busy as a beehive. There were the choir and all kinds of courses and basketball and soccer practice. Now, when you walk through the kibbutz in the afternoon or evening it's like a desert. It's years since a baby was born here. Yet for a long time it looked as if the idea was going to succeed, despite all the difficulties. Like if we could just be patient a little longer, be a little less demanding, the kibbutz would come through all right. It always takes me a couple of days to recover after every visit."

No, I don't really think much about those days. What's the use? But listen, when I compare it to the life of my children today, each has his own room and computer and hi-fi. It was a hard life and we were hard kids. I think what it was, mainly, was that you didn't have the protection of your family. You remember Shmuel, from your brother's class? One day, when he was in third or fourth grade, he discovered that Yanek had got from America sets of first-rate tools—hammers, planes, drills, quality the workers in the joinery never even dreamed of, and that he was keeping them in the old pillbox near the children's livestock farm. Shmuel was a skinny kid, so he'd slip in through the window of that pillbox, borrow a hammer, take it back, borrow another thing, and sometimes didn't put it back. In short, one day the door opened and Yanek came in and Shmuel didn't have time to get away. Now there were some beehives behind the children's livestock farm, remember? So Yanek, who was a neighbor of Shmuel's parents, grabbed him by the hair, dragged him to the hives and shoved his face into one of them. You get it? You know what it means, to push somebody's face into a beehive? Shmuel never set foot outside the house for a whole week, his face was so swollen. But he told me that what upset him worst during that week was not the pain or the humiliation, but the fact that his parents didn't do a damn thing about it. They just waited for the swelling to go down, then sent him back to the children's house.

Okay, so that was exceptional, but by and large life here was tough, and we were tough kids. You remember, when we were in seventh or eighth grade, two huge gray cats turned up in the children's livestock farm and they were killing our chickens. One day me and Shlomo caught one of them in the calves' pen. Shlomo stuck him with a pitchfork, and I tried to finish him off with a hoe. He was incredibly strong. I kept hitting him, and he sank into the cow shit but didn't die. But the funny thing is, all that blood and the smashed head didn't bother me one bit. I tell you, I never gave it a thought afterwards, no dreams or anything. Then, for instance, Shlomo and me and some kids from the class above us used to catch pigeons opposite the cowshed and roast them. You know how we killed them? You hold the pigeon by the head, raise your arm quickly, then slam it down fast—that's it! While waiting for the pigeons to be ready, the popular game was to see how long you could suffocate a chicken without actually killing it. Two of us would hold the chicken by the neck and squeeze. The comb turns blue, the head drops, and the trick is to keep going as long as possible without killing it. If the chicken dies, or you let go too soon, you lose. You didn't know about that, did you? You were busy with other things. But once a week there was a movie in the kibbutz, remember, and right till the end of high school Ozer didn't let us see the movies which had kisses in them, because they'd corrupt us.

Listen, most of our neighbors keep dogs, to guard the yard and the house, but mainly to bother the neighbors at night. Last year we had a gray cat in our yard. Quite nice looking in fact. Two months ago she had kittens, and suddenly we had a big family of cats. My wife liked them, as a matter of fact, until one day the house got full of fleas. And I mean masses! In short, she said we should get rid of the cats. Why? We could spray them. No, she wanted them gone. I said I better take care of it, she'd feel bad if she did. I caught them and put them in the trunk and thought I'd leave them near some garbage dump. Two hours later I was back home with the cats still in the car. My wife got in the car and came back fifteen minutes later, without the cats. Where, how?—Not a word. I'm telling you, maybe these are little things, but we aren't what we used to be either.

A few weeks ago my wife took me to one of those workshops that women go to. I sat and listened, it wasn't anything special. Then after half an hour the moderator asked me to sit opposite my wife and talk to her as if she was my Father, and say to her everything I ever wanted to say to my Father and didn't get a chance. What for? What's there to say that I didn't say? I sat opposite her and thought I'd say a few words and get it over. I thought about my Father and I couldn't say one word. After a minute I simply fell apart. I sat opposite my Father and cried. I blubbed, you know what I mean? And my Father was never such a big thing in my life. That's why I told you, I don't like to think about those days. What for? What good is it?

Singing and Weeping
Early Training

A.

"All right, if there's hot water left I'll have some more tea," Yossi says to Dinah, taking advantage of this exchange with my sister to shed the puzzled boy's expression and resume his adult face. "Let's see, if we discount all the temporary ones, there were six of us kibbutz boys born and bred. So what have we got? One airforce pilot, two generals, two lawyers, one an industrialist, one a school principal who's gone nuts and wants to be mayor, and one poet and professor. Hey, that's not too bad. Are you with me? You're switching off again." I smile at him to show that I'm listening to every word.

B.

My first pigeon was a dead one. One Saturday as I was walking home I saw a gray pigeon lying on the footpath near the big Persian lilac at the approach to the veteran members' houses. It was so light as if it was hollow. Death had taken away its distances and weight.

I was in fourth grade and longed for a dovecote of my own. Elan promised to get me a pair of pigeons for the cote we'd built. Meanwhile I kept chicken fledglings in a couple of cages that Elan helped me to build. When I was in kindergarten I'd brought from the woods a squill bulb, big as a baby's head. I planted it near the outside column of the house and every few days I checked to see if it was striking root. One day I saw that it had put out white roots, thick as earthworms, so I stuck it back in quickly, sensing that I'd intervened in something that should be left to itself. Now the cages stood beside the green squill leaves, and inside the chicks pecked at their food and flapped the tiny wings they were sprouting.

I finished feeding the chicks and hurried to the children's house. Shai and Naomi were waiting for us there, as always on Saturday evenings. Shai was standing with folded arms, rounding us up in his blue eyes. He was holding a green bag on which were printed the red words, De Luxe Coffee, and Nehemiah and I exchanged proud glances: De Luxe. We sat around the campfire we'd prepared in the morning in the empty field behind the basketball pitch. As the fire blazed, it painted our cheeks a warm honey color, the color of ripe wheat. "Lord, let it never end," Naomi's singing voice rose high as can be, and we all flew upward with it.

"Today we'll learn a new song." Naomi's round boyish face was solemn (I'd already noticed that sometimes an ugly girl was a handsome boy). Her slow, steady voice led us through line after line. With her head raised, she leaned back on the melody: "Strike, my hammer, strike again, / on the little nails. / In the house there is naught to eat, / naught but tears and wails." Shai gave us tiny cups of coffee, and Naomi continued to lead us deeper and deeper into poverty-stricken rooms we had never known, dust everywhere, on a low bench a cup of coffee, and a crust of bread, and in the middle sit sad-eyed cobblers, humming the song of poverty. In the second stanza Naomi sang the chorus accompaniment softly, sweetening the sorrow unbearably. Ronni sat opposite me, elbows on knees, hands hanging down, his blue eyes wide open, unfocused. The unfocused gaze left no room for anything but sadness, and only the edge of the eye held a white corner of contentment, because being together, being responsive to suffering, was pleasurable. Our eyes met (for a second I saw myself) and quickly turned away. "City people work for money. To us work itself is a value." Shai's eyes were gray and serious in the flickering firelight. "The principle is simple: each person contributes according to his ability, and receives according to his needs." The symmetrical formula enclosed the life around me, the dining hall and the laundry, the clothing store and the clinic, in a tight frame which held a promise and a consolation. The word "contribute" had the pleasant, secure sound of the brown coin we put every Friday into the JNF box.

"Strike, my hammer, strike again," hummed Batsheva, hurrying to finish the math homework before the end of the break. The charm of the previous evening had not returned.

"You remember that last year we learned about the birds of our country?" Ze'ev asked at the beginning of his class-teacher's hour. I grinned happily. Occasionally I was fortunate enough to be praised for things I liked to do. By the time we learned about birds I already recognized the spotted eggs of the goldfinch and the colibri, the padded lining of the warbler's nest and the wild pigeons' handful of twigs, and Ze'ev made a little display of the abandoned nests I'd brought in a corner of the classroom. "I'm told by the secretariat that there is an infestation of birds in the kibbutz and they have asked us to help get rid of them. So today we'll devote this lesson and the p.t. lesson after it to this issue," Ze'ev said, smiling steadily to sustain the smile that was fading from my lips.

Ronni, Shlomo, and Yossi ran out of the classroom in search of long sticks and ladders, and to make plans. A cold spring sun was shining. Along the track leading to the sheepfold tall thistles protected their heads with purple crowns of thorns. The lambs were scampering from corner to corner, leaping, crashing together in midair, their mouths rounded in a permanent smile. An old memory, a mist of foam or wool, floated before my eyes and sank out of sight, leaving behind a dark emptiness and a thin line of longing. In the cowshed Yehoshua was milking the cows. His gray sweater sleeves were rolled up to his elbows, and the hairy veins of his hands were linked to the rosy veins of the udders. "In another few years you'll be able to milk," he said, smiling. Offended because I did not return his smile, his face became grave. Longing for what?

I walked on to the dining hall and returned to the children's house. The boys came back scratched and excited, carrying dozens of nests and fledglings. Ze'ev suggested they put the fledglings beside the big barrel that stood near our entrance steps. I saw that they were wild pigeon fledglings. Their big bulging eyes were still closed, and their bare reddish bodies were almost transparent. Their heads swayed on long necks, like dolls' heads on springs. Again came the dark hollow and a mist of foam or wool, and a streak of longing.

The fledglings moved closer to each other through the thin grass around the barrel. Two of them touched and raised their open, shrill beaks. A faucet was dripping into the barrel, each drop rounded like an eyeball, then elongated and fell. Something thin, no thicker than the surface of the water, tore inside me at the sight of those naked fledglings, and their yellow cheeping reached me through the tear, like water finding its level in linked vessels.

"What shall we do with these chicks?" Ze'ev consulted us. "We'll manage," said Ronni. Ze'ev went up the stairs and disappeared into the children's house. Ronni looked around. "The girls mustn't look," he said with a wry grin. Shlomo handed him the fledglings, and he threw them one by one at the side of the barrel, as if practicing pitching a ball at the wall. The sparrows in the nearby willow took off as if a shot had been fired. The fledglings fell one after the other at the base of the barrel, their heads slumped, their feet pedaling briefly. Ronni studied at them a moment, the intense sorrow that was awakened by last night's song having turned into a sharp blue shaft. Next time he will strike and strike again with a hammer.

"How can you do such a thing?" asked Ruthie.

"Scoot, girls," I said, and ran to my parents' home.

I was out of breath when I reached the cages that held my chicks. A hollow barrel was roaring in my ears. I opened the doors of the cages, took out the food bowls, slowly closed the doors, soaked bread in water, crumbled it, the fingers working by themselves, detached from me. In one of the cages lay a dead chick, and the others stepped on it as if it were part of the flooring. I removed it, walked away from the house to bury it, then turned around and flung it against the wall of the house, near the big leaves of the squill. But it was so light, such a little bodiless ball of down, that it didn't fly well, only hit the wall and dropped like a flake of plaster, and I didn't hear a thing.

Pampered Children

Yossi's mother—small and thin as a little girl, her scanty hair standing up on her head like a chick's down—knocks on the door and comes in, leaning on the arm of Yossi's wife Drora. She looks around in confusion, spots my mother in the midst of the hubbub, and indicates her presence with a nod, afraid to leave the supporting arm. Dinah hurries to offer her a chair, but she refuses. She says quietly to Yossi, who is bending over her, that she has not visited her husband's grave for a week and wants him to come with her to the cemetery. Yossi gives his wife a brief glance and takes her place beside his mother.

Drora began to study in the comparative literature department at Tel Aviv University two years after me, and I wonder if my image is also permanently associated in her mind with the corridors of the Gilman Building in the late sixties. Like many of the department's graduates, she did not stick to literature and has been working as a journalist for many years. Her graying fair hair is cropped almost to her scalp ("My son calls it the hairstyle of an aging Progressive Party woman," she says, smiling, to my mother), but the skin is still taut on her high cheekbones and her tongue is as brisk as ever.

You've heard that Shlomo has left his wife. Don't ask, it's World War Three. She won't give him a divorce, and he comes over every evening to weep and moan about it. Now I can understand that a husband can stop loving his wife, I can understand that he's in love with another woman, but he shouldn't dump it on us night after night, whining what does his wife want from him, why is she torturing him. The poor thing still loves him, and the schmuck can't figure it out. He ought to accept some responsibility and stop playing the innocent victim. You've no idea what she went through with him till he got established as a lawyer. She survived his thirties crisis and his forties crisis, but she didn't manage to survive his fifties crisis.

My husband? The best there is. He's such a protective father. He's also a great cook. When we're expecting guests he wants the house to shine, so he alone washes the floors. You kibbutz guys were really brought up well. But at the same time, men will be men, what can you do. I know he cares about me, I know he loves me, but right from the start he said it like a set speech, as if—how I shall I put it—as if there is an insulating layer in his chest. A few years ago, when old guys like you were still doing reserve duty, I suddenly got a terrible attack of anxiety before he went. I begged him to ask for a postponement, but he wouldn't. Not that he was so crazy about reserve duty, but he wouldn't change the dates just because of my anxiety. You won't believe this—the day before leaving he went and doubled his life insurance. And he couldn't understand why it made me mad! The hell with the insurance—just bring yourself back in one piece. But that's men all over, isn't it? They understand money, they understand assignments, give them a problem they'll try to solve it. It suddenly struck me that if he can translate my fears into money, perhaps it also works the other way round—that my life insurance will be a fair compensation if anything happened to me. You should see his face when I and the kids give him birthday presents. He has such an embarrassed smile on his face, like a little boy, and I can never figure out if it's because he doesn't know how to show happiness, or because he can't believe that people really love him. Like an orphan who got used to always being alone in the world and not being entitled to anything. . . . There, I can hear them coming back. Give my regards to America, and warn New York we've already booked tickets for the summer.

In the end, Smadar, Batsheva, and Shlomo never arrived. Smadar expressed her condolences on the telephone and promised to try to come to the kibbutz another evening. Yossi, one of few former classmates I'd seen in previous summer vacations, sat beside me at my mother's place, hardly saying a word. Finally he slapped my back, this supposedly experienced mature man, and I, the supposedly experienced man of the world, thanked him for coming.

Crowding

Hairstyles from Overseas

A.

Thursday evening. The living room is packed, as it has been on all the previous evenings. The conversation is typically Israeli: the wonders of Turkey, the poverty of the Indian masses, and the magic of Nepal. Dinah and Elan's friends exchange the names of the countries they have visited, cities and hotels, and evaluate distances and experiences. Though most of them left the kibbutz years ago, there is no mistaking them: their features are carved with a hard, blunt instrument, with no use for subtleties. Many of our parents had a prominent upper lip, like a petulant child. Within one generation they bequeathed to us a peasant's jaw and a heavy, self-assured lower lip. Twenty, thirty years later this peasant look has come to characterize the groups of Israelis who are so unmistakable in the airports of Istanbul, Orlando, or Amsterdam. Having left this narrow place, we have not ceased wandering and flitting about the world. How we managed to pass this wanderlust to the rest of the Israelis, and this need to immediately locate the nearest bathroom (an early sign of claustrophobia), I cannot imagine.

The knock on the door is heard through the general conversation. Brakha comes in. Dinah offers her a chair, but she remains near the door, smiling. She pops in several times a day, to relieve her loneliness. She lost her husband many years ago, and now she would like to school Mom in the art of widowhood. Her complexion is well tended and her long hair is braided like a snail, as though the hairstyle is one of the items carried by immigrants from country to country. Our families lived next door to each other for decades. Every cough, every sigh or reprimand, passed through the dividing wall as if it were an open window. Brakha tells Dinah that she'd forgotten to eat lunch today, and her smile turns into a loud laugh. I remember this laugh well.

B.

We don't fall asleep directly after lights-out. The dark thaws the faces and softens the voices. "My sister told me that after a girl is twelve, she gets blood coming down every month," Batsheva speaks quietly from her bed. Twelve is not very far off now, and I'm surprised that she sounds more curious than anxious. In the dark her stammer is almost unnoticeable. "What about the boys? Does something happen to the boys too?" Yonatan asks from the bed next to mine.

Manya enters the children's house, her brisk footsteps apologizing for her lateness while proclaiming her arrival. Brakha has been doing her turn in the kitchen, and when she enters, her soft soles make almost no noise. Two days ago Father told Mom that Brakha's husband complained that the cookies she had baked were too hard, and she told him to throw them out of the window. Are you crazy, he said, you'll break my roses. Mom said, "We've got to do something, the woman is suffering." Brakha sits down on Yonatan's bed and whispers to him, "Good night." He says there's no need to whisper, nobody is sleeping yet. "What about our neighbor, is he still awake?" she asks, turning to me. I say nothing. Something in her voice alarms me.

"What names do you call each other?" she asks the room in general. "You can call my neighbor an Arab dog," she suggests. "Or you might try, a Romanian thief." She laughs freely, gaily. The first time I was stung by a bee I thought I'd stepped on a thorn or a nail, and was puzzled that the pain did not follow its usual route, but deepened and widened as I kept trying to locate and define it. Now the sting is making my neck swell— lying in the darkness, unmoving, hoping I'm dreaming and that I'll wake from this dream in the morning—and reddens my face.

The epithet "Romanian thief" was promptly forgotten. The kibbutz members walk around even in summer in heavy work boots, and we run around barefoot; the warm earth rumples our hair, roughens and freckles

our skin, and already we are as tall as they. We never thought of ourselves
as Polish or Romanian. We're from the children's house and the children's
livestock farm. How much time do we spend with our parents each day?
At best a couple of hours. And what do I know about my parents' families?
Next to nothing. But an Arab dog is from our fields and orchards, always
with patches of mud or fresh scars on their worn coats. The dogs are cunning and nimble and grab leftover food between showers of stones and
kicks. The first kick came the day after that night, during the school break,
in the middle of a game of marbles. It was followed by another and
another.

Elan and I once brought a pair of pigeon chicks to the dovecote we'd
built. Before evening fell I went up to them quietly: they were sitting side
by side, like a pair of shoes, traces of yellow down still showing on their
gray bodies. Now and then they raised their heads, touched beaks, seeking
food. Visitors who see the expanses of the kibbutz and its lawns have no
idea: amid these green expanses our space is spread between the sixteen
kids of the children's house. Amid the plantations of apples and bananas,
of vineyards and flower beds, we are shoved together between bare walls,
shoving and being shoved, seeking food in each other's empty beak. And
remembering each other's every fault, every weakness. Three years later,
the kids still remembered: I'm an Arab dog. I thought I'd get used to it,
but I didn't. Why was I especially an Arab dog? I've no idea. Who can tell
what was kept in the bundle of grievances and insults that these people
carried with them all the way from Bessarabia and Poland.

There used to be a trough with a row of faucets, as in a summer camp,
at the entrance to the dining hall, and beside it an iron scraper for muddy
boots. This year the faucets have been replaced by a circular room with a
white washbasin in the middle and four silvery taps. Two articles in the
kibbutz newspaper praised the economic committee for the initiative and
the improvement in the quality of our communal life. Fishel comes to
breakfast from the garage where he works, and stands there patiently soap-
ing his hands, the left palm moving like a piston in the right, right hand
slipping into the left, black beads of grease mix with the soap bubbles, his
eyes are rolled up in an expression of innocent humility, informing the
world at large that he's a man of few words, but he's been in the garage
since six A.M., not a second later. Zaitsek the maintenance man, broad as
a hayrick, peers at Fishel's hands and his eyes say, All right, all right, we
know all about you from back in Bessarabia, you don't have to show off.

Shmuel's yellow eyebrows are mussed like rows of wheat after the harvest, his smiling eyes deprecate the mud on his clothes—so what, when you move watering pipes in the fields from morning you're sure to get mucky, no big deal, it may be you or it may be me. Hanoch comes in next, his face has taken on something of the sheep's expression. He soaps and soaps his hands, his strong fingers absorbed in themselves, because a certain sheep has been having a difficult delivery since morning and he won't be here long, will just grab something and go back. The teacher Ze'ev nods good morning without looking left or right, his white hands whispering that the Romanians are the first to arrive again, stealing a few minutes before breakfast. Zvi arrives from the olive grove and gives everyone a good morning through his chapped lips. He washes his short, freckled face and gazes at Shmuel with a resentful look—everyone knows this piece of shit starts the day with the newspaper delivered by the seven o'clock bus. Brakha comes in—you can hardly hear her footsteps on the murky soap stains—her face wearing its permanent apologetic smile, because she's just a little woman whose life is made wretched by her husband. Finally Mom appears. Her face lights up when she sees me, but when she sees Brakha she looks down, because this woman is suffering and something must be done to help her, maybe talk to someone in the social committee, after all.

Pampered Children—Shlomo

Shlomo comes in without knocking—the man of the world, who knows that in times of mourning these niceties may be dispensed with. At school he was near the bottom of the class, took more interest in tractors than in schoolbooks, and was always in the class committee. In the intricate network of friendships and counterfriendships, we were never in the same gang. From newspapers and occasional meetings with old classmates I know about his achievements as a lawyer, though we haven't met since the last class reunion, more than fifteen years ago. His gray hair is as thick as ever, and its careful grooming gives him a senatorial look. He offers a firm hand and says, "I know, I know. Nowadays every phone call makes me jump, I'm so afraid it'll be a call from here to express condolences." He asks about my father's last days, and speaks about his mother's loneliness in the kibbutz. His confident smile demonstrates that he's quite experienced in the customs of bereavement, and only its unsteady edges say, forget it, forget it, it's such a long time ago. He sits down beside Elan, to show that the old class divisions have long ago been obliterated. "The amazing thing is that we all left the kibbutz without a penny, but every one of my kids had a room of his own, and the same is true of your kids and Avram's. I'm willing to bet that all our kids grew up in rooms of their own," he declares combatively, challenging anyone to dispute his assertion.

Four iron beds, a tall wardrobe, and four shelves—mine's the second from the top. My bed stands between the wardrobe and the window, slightly less exposed to the door than the other beds. Nehemiah's and Yehoshua's beds flank the door, and Shlomo's stands along the wall opposite mine. The rain has turned the kibbutz and its fields into a morass, and we don't have to read the notice on the notice board to know we won't be going to work after lunch.

My windcheater was waterlogged when I came into the room. Nehemiah and Yehoshua were already asleep, and Shlomo was lying in bed, reading a sports paper. I tried to warm my feet at the kerosene stove that was burning in the room. Shlomo put the paper down and asked me to be quiet. I lay down on my stomach, my face to the wall, and waited.

Rivka, my brother's classmate, used to wake Noam and Moshe, who slept near her room, at night and ask them to stroke her breasts. Now, with my eyes shut, I saw her walking in the dark to their room, tall, her full breasts too big for her slender body. Moshe took hold of her breasts from behind and turned her to face him. Noam passed a delicate finger from the base of the breast to the nipple and rolled between his fingers. Thinking about the searching hand feeling the warm flesh beneath the blouse gripped my throat. My arms, lying along my body, raised the blanket a little over my back. I turned my head as if to glance casually at the room, and met Shlomo's black eyes watching me with gleeful curiosity.

I turned back to the wall, desire having grown stronger than shame. I was cold. I wanted to be there, enfolded and caressed, carried by the warm currents. Rivka was tired and wanted to go back to sleep, but Moshe blocked her way and Noam again put his hand under her blouse. But Shlomo's breathing behind my back and the strained posture in which I tried to hide my movements, blurred the picture. The three figures slowly dissolved in the dark children's room. I longed to be a hot spark, a tree branch twitching in the fire.

Shlomo rose, put on his shoes and Windbreaker. "I see I won't get any sleep today," he said and went to the door. Then he turned back, pulled out from under his mattress a tattered copy of "My Life and Loves," which had made the rounds of the class, and threw it on the floor beside my bed. I looked up, surprised. His grin was salacious and mocking—it's okay, it's okay, just remember that despite all your Dostoyevskys and all your poetry you're no better than the rest of us—and yet it held a tenderness I'd never seen on his face and didn't know he had in him. "It's okay," he said quietly and shut the door behind him. His grin hung in the air for a long time, like that of the Cheshire cat.

Pampered Children
Sex Is Little Moments of Love

I compliment Smadar on her dress (a white silk shirt with big, mannish pockets, tailored brown slacks), and she laughs: "I have to look good, for his sake." Her page-boy hairstyle frames a somewhat scorched complexion, which proves that it is easier to leave the kibbutz than to change the face it gave its children. Her father is lying in the kibbutz nursing unit, and once a week she drives over from Herzliya, where she works for a hi-tech company. Once, when we were children, we saw a fifty-lira note in the room of one of the members. I don't remember who he was, or why we were in his room, or even the high-denomination bill lying on the table, only the look she and I exchanged when we returned to the kindergarten, agreeing without a word not to tell the others where we'd seen the money, to avoid implicating its owner. Almost half a century has passed since then, and for a long time money has not been something to be ashamed of in the kibbutz. "You remember the fifty-lira bill?" I ask her, and she shakes her head. We have rarely seen each other since we left the kibbutz, more than thirty years ago, yet the conversation flows as if we met yesterday. "That's how it is in a family," she says, her smile cracking her sunburnt face.

No, I never had nightmares. If I remember anything, it's a certain insecurity. Nurses came and went, and by the time you became attached to one, you had to start getting used to another. There was nothing to hold on to. I look at my own daughters—right into their teens they still took a teddy or a scruffy old doll to bed with them. We never had such teddy bears or dolls, and the few toys in the kindergarten belonged to everyone. But I can tell you that I soon grew a sort of inner muscle. Let's say they've just told us that tomorrow there will be a new nurse, or a new teacher. At first it sounds real frightening, because you've no control over what's happening, you don't know this new woman and what to expect from her. So to reassure myself, I'd make a list of the things that were not going to change: I'll still be living in the same room with Nehemiah and Ronni and Avigdora, after supper I'll still go home till bedtime, and on Friday they'll still give us pants, shirt, and underwear for the week, at breakfast and supper we'll still eat an egg and salad, and all that sort of thing. In moments of anxiety this muscle immediately went into action. Also, quite early on I invented a sort of quick balance sheet. Like, for instance, the new nurse doesn't know that I wet my bed till I was in first grade, or she's a neighbor and friend of my parents. You know, I'm often amazed by the difference between my feelings for my daughters and my feelings for my sister's children. For a long time I thought it meant I was a bad, selfish woman. Then I understood that for her children I have this kind of muscle, but not for my girls. Today it's not even a muscle any more, just a kind of practicality. When anything happens, big or small, my first thought is, how does it affect me. Will it change my life. If it doesn't, I can live with it.

In the company where I work I had to train myself to show an interest in people. When they asked me how I was, I had to make myself ask them how they were. I don't know exactly how it's connected, but there you are—it wasn't easy for me to tell someone that I love him. I had to overcome a thousand barriers. In the end I understood that Marx was right: sex is little moments of love. It wasn't Marx? All right, so it's my definition. At least they taught us to speak plainly, without fancy stuff, didn't they? At least we came out of it strong, down-to-earth sort of people.

Pampered Children—Batsheva

Batsheva! I recognize her at once—Batsheva, of course, who else. But this familiarity is soon dispelled, and I realize that I wouldn't have known her if I passed her in the street. Memory overcame the time gap since our last meeting, but only momentarily, it linked the present face with the past and immediately left off. The passage of years puffed out her face, spaced out her teeth, and gave her hair a dun color. A minute or two later I couldn't tell which features my eyes had captured that made for a certain recognition when she stood in the doorway.

I can well recall her round, orderly handwriting and the soapy drops that fell slowly from the long black hairs that had suddenly sprouted between her legs. She was the first to grow breasts, and until the shared showers ended, in sixth grade, she used to wash herself quickly under the shower, a strained smile on her face. She was the boys' favorite, with her rolling laugh and the slight stammer that softened the beauty of her blue eyes. The old photographs don't reveal her beauty—knowing that only one photograph was taken of each child made her nervous and tense, and at the moment the picture was taken she always grimaced, and so the photographs captured her stammer. I heard a rumor that she married late (Any children? After all those shared years, how little we know about each other today). She has been working as a teacher in Givatayim and is fed up; I shouldn't ask how fed up she is with the work.

Her parents died years ago, and she comes to the kibbutz every month or two, to see her sister, a classmate of Elan's. She speaks slowly, as if she's pushing a heavy wagon. If you didn't know that as a child she used to stammer, you wouldn't notice a thing.

What amazes me, when I think about our childhood, is the members' conviction that we were a clean slate on which they could write whatever they saw fit. So they wrote on us: be brave and not afraid of the dark and the jackals, and be the very opposite of everything we hated about our parents and ourselves. We won't actually be your parents, but please love us as a child loves his parents. And above all, be loyal to the kibbutz and to the movement. And they were naive enough, or stupid enough, to believe that this is what would happen. How they chucked us, aged two or three, into a children's house that was the furthest building in the kibbutz, right by the fence. You remember that poem—"Wizened and quiet, my mother laid me down by the fence"—it was read out on some occasion in school, and for a moment I thought it was a poem about me.

What I do remember is the constant feeling that our everyday activities were only a kind of preparation, that we were little soldiers training for a terrifying future. You remember how seriously they trained us in second grade to jump from the roof onto a stretched blanket that the whole class held tight down below? Maybe the boys enjoyed it, but for me in fourth grade sliding on an omega from the water tower was sheer terror. I don't mean just the fear of jumping down to the blanket, or sliding on an omega, I mean the sense that it was all a preparation for a future in which you'll need to use these skills or you'd be lost.

The way we lived here was like a religious order, or a military camp. No wonder you guys did so well in the army. Everything had its code, everything was symbolic—the hairstyle and the length of the pants and the color and material of the clothes, and what time you got up in the morning and went to bed at night. It's really weird—on the one hand, we were apparently perfectly free, almost without adult supervision, almost neglected, and at the same time we lived under a cloud of written and unwritten rules. There was a strong feeling that everything you do is recorded somewhere, that you're always picking up merits or demerits. I remember you, near the end of high school, coming into the dining hall one evening with your sleeves turned up to the elbows. You were always the imaginative sort, weren't you. And when you walked to your table the members looked at you with indignation, as if you were breaking a law, because here we wear either long or short sleeves. Only city people, or people in movies, turn up their sleeves like this. So observe the rules, please!

Anyway, you didn't stand a chance here. You were quick, nimble. David Ofer, who was in charge of the cotton fields, complained that he could barely harvest in a whole day as much as you did in a couple of hours in the afternoon. But people here admired power. Who can lift a bale of hay highest, or carry a whole stem of bananas all the way to the end of the row, and the boys were always competing in weight lifting or Indian wrestling. When the members of Mishmar David came to visit on some holiday, or maybe to celebrate it with us, there was Indian wrestling at the end, remember? Then someone suggested a competition between their strongest guy and ours, and the whole dining hall buzzed with excitement. The table where they held the contest was surrounded with dozens of young guys and nobody could get closer. The holiday atmosphere, the declamations and dances that were scheduled for that evening—everything came down to two thick forearms. You, with your turned up sleeves, you never had a chance here. Most of our class came back to the kibbutz after the army, until we began to scatter all over the country, one after the other. Here too you showed originality, so I wasn't surprised when I heard that you told the secretariat you were leaving, even before you finished your military service. In those days I was sure I'd never have the guts to pick up and leave, and I was glad for you.

Singing and Crying
Homeland Songs

A.

The prolonged stay in my childhood kibbutz is turning me into a flute in which all the songs of my childhood keep resounding. Not only the songs of the War of Independence and the Suez War ("A song about a tree, a lone tree, a sycamore swaying in the wind," sang Yaffa Yarkoni in our culture hall immediately after the war, and a soldier whom she invited up from the audience stared at her, mesmerized), but also songs of Pentecost and Tu Bishvat, which I hadn't realized were stored in my memory. "In the city and the village, children up and toil, carrying to hill and dale plantings for the soil," I am marching with the other kindergarten kids to the Tu Bishvat planting. In a moment my cypress sapling will tilt sideways, and Father will show me how to do it. "Sow and plant, plant and sow," the words draw one another along; I'm merely the hollow tube through which they pass.

Friday, the fourth day of the shivah. "Bab el-Wad, remember forever our names!" Since morning I've been hearing Mom singing inside me, again and again, till her voice faded and only the melody lingers through the day. Aryeh Asa, the music teacher who came to the kibbutz every Tuesday, taught us this song when we were in fourth grade, and after the first couple of lines the chatting and laughter and throwing of paper planes ceased. The armored convoys to Jerusalem had left from our woods, we saw their burnt-out shells on our annual trip to Jerusalem, and the melody seeped into us like water into the soil and raised delicate flowers of sorrow.

This sorrow brought me closer to myself, the way a wound or a pain brings one closer to oneself, and at the same time submerged me entirely in the singing group. I felt the same dual sense of intensified, solemn, burnished selfhood combined with total self-oblivion, in the following lessons in which Aryeh taught us "On the banks of the Dnieper," "We'll build our country," "Laugh at my dreams," and other favorite homeland songs. At home Mom's voice caressed the words of the songs, and Father drew out and elongated the notes, humming and quavering the phrases (he managed to turn even the marching song, "We'll build our country," into a quavering Hassidic melody).

In the following years we often sat with our youth movement counselors around the campfire, and the glow of its flames kneaded all our features and gave us all identical faces, the faces of self-sacrifice, sorrow, and longings, as if speech was individually located in each person, while the songs held the same place in everyone. The children's house was a permanent training ground for restraint and dissimulation. These songs were a valve through which we could safely pour out our hearts, and through them we channeled all our joys and the sorrows of our youth. Right from the first song, without any preliminaries, under our normal voices—the voices of the children's house, school, and dining hall—another voice could be heard, caressing the melody, growing finer and finer, misting our eyes with a faraway look. The flesh, too, grew finer and purer, filling with a secret longing to become spirit. "Once more the song sets forth, once more our days weep as they pass. Caravan, where are you heading? Caravan, the roads are sad." Once more the song sets forth, and again I feel the misty gaze (shrinking under the pressure of memory rising from deep in the cranium), and the flood of longings in my chest.

Memories and longings go hand in hand. What then did I long for in my childhood? Surely not for the first five years of my life. "Five years passed for Michael / in song and in dance. / No work had he, nor any schooling. / Three friends had he: / a dog, a cat and in the cote a dove." Batya the nurse taught us this song when we were in kindergarten, and I hesitated to join the singing, afraid that this new wistful plaything would be abruptly taken away. The songs I had known so far were songs of the soil or national songs, as well as of the festivals of Hanukkah, Pentecost, and Tu Bishvat. This new song held a strange yearning. The atmosphere in the children's house and at my parents' discouraged complaints and tears, encouraged self-control and strength of character, and here a simple, recurring melody invoked sadness and longing I didn't know were in me, and I felt them shaping my expression. I hesitated to surrender to the sweet sorrow, for fear that it would vanish for good, but every additional line that Batya taught us in her high voice only deepened Michael's sadness at parting from his carefree childhood. No one scolded me for this sorrow, and I could expand and deepen it indefinitely when we put the separate lines together and sang the whole song for the first time.

"Five years passed for Michael / in song and in dance." I shut my eyes and realize with great clarity: yes, that is how it began. The homeland songs Aryeh taught us some years later in the music lessons found us quite ready. The battles and the fallen mentioned in those songs intensified the sorrow, and the more it grew, the greater the joy. The greater the sadness, the more beautiful we became in our own eyes, convinced that people are measured by the degree of sadness they have in them. We grew up between the walls of the children's houses, among fields that were laid out in squares of alfalfa and wheat, olive and apple orchards and banana plantation, and these melodies, which hinted at the loneliness of endless roads, the whistling of the vast Russian plains, imprinted on us their sweet longing and sadness. We didn't stand a chance against them—as though the mighty Dnieper had burst into the narrow course of the River Jordan and obliterated it under its flood.

Ozer Huldai, the principal of the local school, used to boast that the kibbutz had resolved to avoid lessons of indoctrination. Nowadays I wonder if he was being naive or disingenuous. Those songs molded us at will, implanted in us strange longings and alien loves, and attached us to the great family of children returning to their motherland and promising her liberty and eternal loyalty. The music lessons, in which we learned to sing the songs and play them on the recorder, were supposedly a slight, unconsidered diversion from the real lessons, namely, algebra and English, chemistry and history. Who would have guessed that in the final analysis, these songs would be the only provision we'd carry away from those long years of study.

B.

(Notes for a lecture about youth movement songs, delivered at the Bait Israel synagogue, April 1997)

Let us start with Haim Gouri's song, "Bab el-Wad":

> Here I pass and stop beside the stone,
> Black asphalt road, rocks, promontories.
> Slowly evening falls, a sea breeze blows,
> A first star gleams over Bait Mahsir.
>
> Bab el-Wad,
> For ever our names recall!
> Convoys broke through to the city!
> Beside the road lie our dead,
> The iron hull as silent as my comrades.
>
> Bab el-Wad . . .
>
> And as I walk past, quietly,
> I remember every single one;
> Here we fought together on the rocks,
> Here we were one family, we all.

This song, and the others in your hands, are an Israeli identity card, the identity of everything we dreamed of being. In it, we were "always ready for the call," and "what more can you ask of us, O Motherland." We are the brave-browed lads, as yet unmarred by evil. Sing this song with any of my classmates, and at once you'll see the misty look, like an inner call to rally around the flag, like a conditioned reflex.

I don't call it a conditioned reflex in mockery, but to emphasize its power. The power stems from its capacity to seize Israeliness by the scruff. What are the essential characteristics of this Israeliness? First of all, the fact that it was created in a struggle, against all the odds. Other songs in the collection before you reveal the stages of this struggle: the rejection of life in the diaspora, immigration to Israel despite many obstacles, the urge to conquer the desert and the swamps, and the struggle with the Arabs. You will see how often the word "liberty" recurs in these lines, and the numerous nouns and adjectives used to express the unity of the participants in the struggle. The desperation and lack of choice that underlay this struggle greatly intensified their sense of Israeliness.

Native Israeliness absorbed the intensity of a life-and-death struggle. But it was not only the struggle that shaped the particular character of this identity. After all, many other countries achieved independence after a prolonged struggle. We find other reasons in the core of the song: "Here we fought together on the rocks, / Here we were one family, we all." "One family" means companionship and comradeship in arms, and all that they imply. Moreover, this comradeship offered an alternative to the family they did not really have. Only one of all my classmates in the kibbutz had grandparents. All the rest had abbreviated families: parents and one or two siblings. And the parents, too, were with us only a very small part of the time. In town, parents were more in evidence, but there too the families were often minimal—parents and their children. In the first place, the pioneers who came here had left their families behind in Europe, and secondly, the boys who took part in the fight for the State of Israel detached themselves quite early from their families.

The place of the biological family was taken by a much bigger one. Look over the collection and you will see how often the poet addresses the homeland as mother. This identification of mother and homeland (an obvious influence of Russian songs) voiced the yearnings of the pioneers who came to Eretz Israel, and was a satisfying expression for the spirit of the young people born there. The line "Here we fought together on the rocks" plays on the dual meaning of the preposition: we fought "on" those rocks to break the siege of Jerusalem, but also "for" each and every rock. Other songs in this collection also express love for the soil of the homeland. In the absence of family and the genealogical continuity that tie a person to a place, Mother-Homeland takes their place, and every battle casualty becomes another root in the ground. Thus the missing families were replaced by two alternatives: first, the family of the fighters, the road builders and swamp drainers; second, the children of this family are also the sons returning to the bosom of their mother, to plow her fields and protect her home.

The identification of homeland and mother suited the purpose of the kibbutz educators and the leaders of the youth movements: it was the shortest way to forge a bond between the generations, to create an illusion of family where there was none, an illusion of roots in a place of sand and rocks. And these songs certainly fulfilled their purpose: all the schoolchildren in my native kibbutz, who learned these songs and sang them in youth movement meetings, parties, and holidays, are living in Israel today. Our children, however, are scattered all over the world. I can testify that, as a child growing up in the kibbutz, in kindergarten or school, I was a complete outsider. Yet when I sang these songs I was a faithful, enthusiastic kid, in no way set apart from the singing group, a total Israeli, confident of his strength and the justice of his cause. In retrospect, I am amazed by what a huge part of me was this Israeli identity—as though I was first of all an Israeli, and only secondly an individual child with his own personality. In recent years I find myself often dreaming about my youth in the kibbutz. It is hardly even a dream—more an outburst of longing, like a torrent of weeping, a prolonged wail. For a long time I failed to understand these longings, because I had never, from my earliest days, felt at ease in that place. Today I am clearer about which part of me is pining like this.

Read "Bab el-Wad" once more and you will see that there is no trace of ambivalence in it as to the justice of the Israeli cause. The Israeli soldiers are the good and the brave, right is on their side, whereas those who oppose them are the evil ones, threatening the integrity of the family. Again on a personal level, I can testify that that was how we were brought up. We were convinced that we were wholly justified in our conflict with the Arabs, and that we were special, beautiful, and wonderful.

At school and in the youth movement we talked endlessly about the value of the individual and freedom of choice, and sang wholeheartedly the songs before you. While growing into adults we made the astonishing discovery that we did not see reality as individuals, but as a chorus, for whom the words and the music had been precomposed. What is worse, we thought that we alone sang our longings for this land, only to find that others had likewise composed and sang to it. Maturation brought the painful realization that two victims had struggled for this land, and one of them was our doing. The total conviction of being in the right, which had been such an essential component of our Israeli identity, was undermined. And still, it is hard to detach oneself from those songs, because in them we are still wonderful and just and together. Detaching oneself is so difficult, because it means, among other things, to lose the family you never had.

Consider the power of this combination of youth and its yearnings, the terrors of war and the joy of victory, in a struggle for a homeland which is also Mother. Consider the inevitable awakening from these youthful dreams, from a world in which everything was either black or white, and you will understand that for me and for many of my generation to be an Israeli means to have been expelled from the womb twice. And the second time not when you're a helpless newborn, but a grown person. Indeed, the second expulsion can only take place when one is an open-eyed grown-up. It is an unending expulsion. Even one who has awakened, has done so only partially. Deep inside, one is still a part (or strives to be a part, grieves at not being a part, refusing to be torn away) of this "one family."

(If there's enough time: distinguish between those who took part in the events and long for past times, and my generation, who had the longings implanted in them by means of the songs. In fact, they were too nostalgic for times they never knew. Is it then in the nature of such emotions to pine for what never was? Always at secondhand?

If questions are asked about the suffering and injustice we have inflicted, quote Martin Buber's distinction between injustice and crime.)

Coffee

Friday night. The hubbub of visitors is over, the cups are washed and dried, and Mom is sitting at the table, exhausted. I put my hand on hers, to say that everything will be all right, and she nods wearily, pretending to believe me. "Did I have a happy life here? There were happy moments. One day Father brought a few sackfuls of gravel, I don't know where from, and poured it on the ground inside the tent. Suddenly it was bright inside. And then there was the war. It's a funny thing to say, but we had been training for wartime. I don't know if you can call it happiness, but there was a wonderful feeling in the midst of all the distress. And we were right at the front! But fear brought us together more than the socialist ideas, and you felt that you were doing something, that you mattered. You know how it is—on important days, for instance, a wedding day, everything that happens, every word you say or you hear, seems full of significance, symbolic. That's how it was. The whole time was both mourning and wedding.

"One of the first times I went to a Gordonia meeting, a representative from Eretz Israel talked to us about two kinds of happiness—happiness when you obtain something, and happiness when you succeed in clearing your mind of all desires or wishes. We became quite enthusiastic when he said that we would be those who achieve something in an active way, those who turn dreams into reality. But here in the kibbutz, after the war, there was no question of realizing things, only of managing in time. Get supper done in time, get breakfast done in time, get all the linen and clothes laundered in time, make sure the children get up and go to school in clean clothes, and that in winter they'll all have sweaters and rubber boots that fit. Was I happy here? Sometimes, on festivals and celebrations there was a feeling that we were a big family. But it generally took a long time. Years after I finished looking after a particular group, when I remembered how I went with them on the annual trip, or how they looked in the graduation party, or how the boy that I got as a skinny, sniffly child finished secondary-school big and strong, so that the army uniform looked tight on him—well, years later I could feel something that you can call happiness."

When I was a boy I would sometimes go home on Friday nights after supper and have coffee with Mom and Father. I can well remember the bitter grains of coffee that floated on the milk, and the thin glass cups, engraved with a delicate, transparent sprig. The coffee was too hot ("By the time it reaches your children's house it's already cool," Father said, proud of his ability to drink it piping hot), and very sweet. And it always aroused an obscure expectation. More than once I asked Mom to make this coffee for me during the week, hoping vaguely that it would somehow fulfil its hidden promise. But to taste the particular flavor of disappointment associated with this coffee you had to drink it late on Friday evening, dressed in a white shirt, with the ease of knowing that tomorrow is a day off from school and work. It had to be drunk in the hope that Mom and Father would also sit at the table and something would be said, at long last, something would happen, or change, or become clear, or perhaps a visitor would come and bring a new spirit.

Sometimes there was a moment of harmony: Mom would stop tidying the place and sit down heavily at the table, and Father would put down the newspaper, and we would sit at the table with the cups of hot coffee and the cookies Mom had baked. Just for a moment we were outside the checkerboard of the kibbutz timetable, and in the bubble of peace which momentarily enclosed the table, life held the sweetness of the hot milk. The glass cups and bright silver teaspoons were unlike the heavy dishes and silverware used in the dining hall, and hinted at a world in which everything was solemn, precise and practical, generous, spacious and self-sufficient. Friday night came, and I'd head for home with a vague expectation of something that never was and would never return.

A Dream

Saturday morning, the fifth day of the shivah. I'd had a dream that night: I am again in sixth or seventh grade, in the children's house in which we lived till we finished primary school. It was night, and Israel was attacked by Arab gangs and defeated. In my dream the war took the form of a night exercise on the hills around the kibbutz. Against all expectations, the Arabs were not afraid of the dark and did not run away from our attacks, but continued their assaults with the cunning of hoodlums. I was hindered from the start of the war by a feeling of weightiness; I struggled through the fields as though they were a quagmire. Elan, a big boy by then and responsible for carrying ammunition from one side of the kibbutz to the other, stared at me in surprise and ran on. His head was visible in the dark for a moment, then he fell into the trap the Arabs had laid for him. The lines of the Jews suddenly collapsed, like a circle of weary dancers, and from afar came volleys of shots accompanied by screams and crying. Someone grabbed me from behind in the hollow darkness, and a shiver of terror paralyzed me.

Strange, how this sojourn in my childhood kibbutz is bringing back the old nightmares. The first time I had this dream, shortly after the Suez War, I dreamed that Ze'ev, our class teacher, summoned us to an emergency meeting. He informed us about the defeat, and promised that nothing would change in our life, except that from now on Israel would be under Arab occupation. His eyes were cast down, and we avoided looking at each other: those ragged, pockmarked types, who could hardly pronounce a complete sentence, had actually won. Lusha the nurse, calling out that it was a quarter to seven, broke the somber silence in the class. In the noise of children getting up and dressed the paralyzing fear dissipated and the details of the battle were forgotten. Only the sense of awful humiliation never left me all day.

In later years the dream became more intricate. When I'd learned to wake myself in the middle, the dream cunningly acquired a second layer. I'd dream that I woke up and found that this time it was not a dream but reality: Israel had been conquered by the Arab states. The dream stipulated that my life in the kibbutz would continue as before, but nevertheless it always caused me acute anxiety and a sense of humiliation which stayed with me for hours. When the school principal presented us with the question if we were Israelis or Jews, my answer was ready. I knew that to be an Israeli meant first of all being independent, or more precisely: determined to achieve independence despite all obstacles. Wasn't that what the songs were all about?

The thought about the Israeli in me created a subtle link between me and my classmates, and was very reassuring. But this reassurance did not last. At night I'd sit alone in the reading room of the culture hall, full of the passionate self-pity of adolescence, trying to dispel my loneliness with smoke. A poem I wrote on one of those evenings had Tarzan complaining about his loneliness in the forest, "Deadlier than a snake, fiercer than a tiger." I read Schopenhauer, who compared the individual's desire for the company of other men to the vain attempt of a hedgehog to approach others of its kind. I imagined a palm of prickly-pear groping towards others like it. Now and then I'd get up and spin around, trying to wind an invisible rope around myself.

Parting

Many of our friends, unable to come to the kibbutz during the week, came on Saturday evening. When we were children, that was how we visited sick classmates who were lying at home, at their parents' place. The visits would begin quietly, with self-conscious politeness, and as we got used to the parents' presence, would turn into giggles and jokes we believed rude. In my parents' house things went differently: talk and laughter were slow and joyless, like a bonfire made with damp faggots. Lying on Mom's bed, I created an atmosphere of chilly embarrassment. I was too much in need of love to be able to respond to it. After forty years, that embarrassment has congealed and learned to hide behind a phony maturity. Dinah listened, amused, to the stories and jokes, and it was evident that she still missed that companionship.

"No one got enough love in the children's house," I said to her a couple of hours later. The guests had left, Mom had gone to bed, and Dinah and I, a trained team, washed and dried the dishes. "For some reason, both you and I had a specially strong need of love, as if our lives depended on it. You could see in our eyes the belief that extra sensitivity and extra loneliness entitled us to extra privileges. We saw in the children's livestock farm how the weaker hen got to eat last, but we wanted to compel the world to bend its laws for us."

"There was so much injustice here," said Dinah. "No, it wasn't right," she added thoughtfully, unable to discard the kibbutz vocabulary which clung to a reality that might have been.

My last years in high school were spent in splendid isolation. I'd stay till midnight in the reading room of the culture hall, filling my head with cigarette smoke, Yehuda Amichai's loves and wars, and inhaling Schopenhauer's bitter ideas. Whenever we had to go to Tel Aviv, to see the dentist or for some other treatment, we were given a little spending money to buy falafel or a soda. I saved this money and bought my first book—Yehuda Amichai's *Two Hopes Away*. After I'd published a poem in the children's paper, Yosef Evven, our literature teacher, suggested that I should read Amichai's poems. Until that time, I'd known only Bialik's and Chernikhovsky's poems, which were taught in literature lessons. Those poems were part of the chorus of voices which called on me morning, noon, and night to be a good boy and a hardworking student, to take part in the committees of the children's society, to edit its newspaper and act as counselor to the kids from sixth grade and from the immigrant settlements that had sprung up not far from Hulda. On the bus back from Tel Aviv, I opened the Amichai book at random and read:

> For the thirty-second time I've put on the world
> and still it doesn't fit.
> It weighs on me,
> not like this coat, which has taken my form,
> feels comfortable
> and will wear out.

The words tickled me—the analogy between life and a coat, at first alluded to and then explicit, and the surprise in the final line—and I laughed with pleasure. Amichai tossed up the words between his hands, threw them up in the air, then caught them and put them back in a new and unexpected order. There was something enigmatic about them, but the puzzle exactly fitted my capacity for solving it. So these lines told me not only about Amichai's life, but about the particular phase in my own life, affirmed my existence and delighted me no end.

Sitting at night in the reading room, I'd turn on a single lamp over my armchair—the dark room was the nearest thing to the bohemian garrets of Paris, which I had read about in Balzac's and Victor Hugo's novels. And so I sat in the kibbutz garret, drowning my solitude in Amichai's loves and Schopenhauer's pessimistic loneliness. Right through high school, Fridays were devoted to the study of psychology and philosophy. I shall always be grateful to the principal for not trying to raise us as somnolent peasants, either because he believed that kibbutz people should know something of Kant and Marx, or because he had not worked out what kind of personality he wished us to have. In this way I became acquainted with Freud and Schopenhauer, the two luminaries of my youth. The culture hall was surrounded by lawns, and a little further away stretched the green rectangles of the orange grove, the orchards of apples and pears. At school the walls bore illustrated slogans that preached a healthy soul in a healthy body, and I filled my head with smoke and Schopenhauer's description of the world as an evil and an agony from which death alone liberates. I was a country boy. The Bible teacher brought his family over from the town of Netanya to the kibbutz, and his wife, who worked as a substitute nurse, showed me one day how to eat with knife and fork. I was alarmed: outside the kibbutz lay a different world, whose rules I did not know. I had one pair of high work boots which I wore to school, as well as to work in the cowshed and the sheepfold, which I polished before festivals and weddings, and wore in the evenings in the reading room, when I sauntered alone in the strange landscapes I found in Freud and Schopenhauer. My mental muscles were strained to the maximum, and the effort was so liberating because Freud and Schopenhauer drew a negative picture of the world of words, the world of "positive" and "negative" kids, in which I lived during the day, and did so—what a relief!—without guilt or hypocrisy. In those evenings I first experienced the pleasure of discovery (a physical pleasure, like that of the taste buds' first experience of a new fruit), of the concentrated mind rereading a text twice and three times, adapting to its rules and starting to examine its surroundings and form early connections: Schopenhauer's Nirvana and Will as trailblazers to the principle of pleasure and the Id.

There stood on my parents' bookcase a bottle filled with layers of variously colored sand that my brother Elan had brought from a class trip to Eilat. I came to understand, courtesy of Arthur Schopenhauer, that I too was made up of a stack of layers: a "sabra," a child of a kibbutz, an Israeli, a male, a high-school student, one of the sixth batch of the kibbutz's children, and my parents' son. Mom used to come home late from work, her back aching, and often asked me to untie her shoelaces. I always felt an obscure reluctance as I crouched in front of her and undid the laces of the shoes which had taken the shape of her feet. "Don't bother, if it's so hard for you," Mom said once, and I assured her it was not hard at all. Some hours later, in my dark garret, Schopenhauer explained that the sense of individuality is a mere delusion, and thereby solved a difficult puzzle: the one who found it hard to untie his mother's shoelaces was the kibbutz boy, for whom the posture of a servant totally contradicted everything he had been taught in his sixteen years in the kibbutz.

It was strange to think about that entity within me, yet I felt comfortable with that kibbutznik. He was like a big brother, one to rely on and be proud of, and moreover it relieved me of much of the responsibility for my actions. But I also felt cheated: the black shock of hair, which I had taken such pains to cultivate (for weeks I and my classmates slept with kerchiefs on our heads, to make our hair conform to the desired shape), was suddenly alien, not mine, not myself. And if I am but a heap of layers stuffed into me by the nurses and teachers, who is the person thinking this thought, who is it who feels his loneliness like a rope around his neck? I was confused.

One entity that I discerned in me served as a starting point for searching other figures. It was easy to distinguish the thrusting male in me. This male choked with desire before the mysterious bodies of the girls (the eyes never ceasing trying to penetrate the soft purses in which they kept their gold). Schopenhauer had taught me how independent (not a kibbutznik, not an Israeli—a distinctive identity by itself) this being was. The billy goats we raised in the children's livestock farm were yellow and stinking with lust in the mating season. Seeing the goats leaving for the pasture they'd raise their heads over the fence of their pen and stick out their tongues in a long despairing baa. During the summer boys and girls did the milking together in the shed, and on specially hot days the girls would take off their shirts, remaining in their bras. The torrid air was heavy with the odors of sheep turds and squirts of milk, and I felt the bitter male cry in my throat.

At sixteen we all got our identity cards, and I distinctly felt that mine was blank. I felt my eyes alter their gaze when facing people: a wide-open, disingenuous, self-effacing gaze before the girls; a strained, somewhat reserved and concentrated gaze before the boys; bashful and awkward before Shlomit, Elan's beautiful classmate; and always reflective— returning an innocent gaze to an innocent one, unfocused to the unfocused, reserved to the reserved. I felt myself chafing against the walls of the children's house, in the cowshed and the sheepfold, breathing the air of the kibbutz and of the fields and plantations all around, expanding and shrinking, growing alternately thicker and thinner, leaving traces of myself in every contact with the trees and houses. Though the inner emptiness was filled with warm pride when I came first in the hundred-meter dash and the high jump during the traditional May Day celebration, anger or a reprimand could knock me off my base, as though I had no weight of my own.

One Saturday I sat on a bench near the dining hall to wait for Elan, and meanwhile observed the people who went in to lunch or came out slowly after the meal. They turned to each other, chatted and laughed, drew near and separated. In the sunlight these dense movements looked to me like the lines of an intricate geometric structure. By the time Elan arrived I had the outline of my graduating assignment in psychology ready in my mind: every person is a vector with his or her own individual quantity, direction, and color. The quantity determines the power relations between given individuals (who will approach whom, who will open a conversation with whom, who will laugh at whose joke). Freud speaks of the human being as a closed system whose character is largely determined by the tension between its component parts. In fact, the system is not closed at all, or closed only for short, localized periods. And just as the mixture of different colors produces different hues, so do we vary greatly in different situations and combinations. Freud discussed the child who wanted to turn the family room into a bedroom, but did not describe the constantly changing flow of the dining hall. The remark that the teacher Yeheskel wrote at the end of my paper—"These statements are fine and true, but a great deal has already been written about this"—confounded me the same way as when I was first shown how to eat with knife and fork: there was a world outside the kibbutz which I knew nothing about. But the basic problem remained. I too was branded, like our cattle: a "sabra," an Israeli, a kibbutz child. Where was I behind those labels?

As for loneliness, I tried with all my might to apply Schopenhauer's edict: "To be happy one must be entirely free, self-sufficient." In 1962 I spent Purim Eve in a dark field opposite the kibbutz gate. From afar I could see the lights of the celebration in the culture hall, and I withdrew further into the darkness. Once when I was three I went with Father to feed the hares he was raising near the kibbutz fence. Beyond the fence the clover field glistened with dew and looked like a calm green lake that invited rolling and snuggling and getting lost in it. I ran toward it as fast as my little legs carried me, and dropped into it as into a huge womb. But the stiff clover stalks scratched me and stained my clothes, and my father's scolding added insult to injury. Now too the night was alien and hostile and I found no comfort in the prickly hay and the disembodied eyes that hovered like fireflies at a distance. Very deliberately I looked up and gazed at the starry skies, and for a moment I felt the fist clamped on my diaphragm relax a little. But the lights of the culture house and the party sounds from afar were stronger than anything. Several times on my way back I spun round and round, like a bundle of straw being tied up.

Near the end of the school year I found in the mailbox of the children's society a letter addressed to me from the literary editor of the Labour daily, *Davar:*

"Moshe Ben-Shaul has forwarded to me some poems you sent to *Young Ma'ariv.* He felt that *Davar* would be a more suitable venue for them. Unfortunately, you sent the poems in handwriting and inaccurate vowelization, which made some of the lines difficult to read. I am sending you the poems, typed and vowelized, hoping I have interpreted your intentions correctly. Yours, Ezra Sussman."

Self-Portraits

Some people's faces wear a child's wonder.
Their wonder is a pliant thing:
Mirror-like, it reflects whatever
It encounters,
Grief or bewilderment.
Their wide-open eyes
Cannot speak firmness
Or assurance.

Some people's faces wear a world wonder.
These have but little joy:
The moan coming from the street,
Sounds of people and dogs,
Rise in them, resistless,
As in linked vessels.

The cord, it seems, that tied them to the world
Never did heal, was never weaned.

Stubborn and desperate
They still reach out to it—
Forever aliens, forever set apart.

Lonelier Than a Snake or a Tree

Tarzan was contented.
He spent his days serenely.
Embracing a tree,
Wrestling with a beast,
He felt the world's living heart.
But he did know dark moments.
Suddenly the forest was
A mass of looming trees and fangs.
Suddenly the loneliness
Was deadlier than a snake,
Fiercer than a tiger.
Where are they now,
My school companions,
Army comrades,
Fellow students,
Bereaved, he growled among the trees.
Alarmed, he found,
Nothing could take their place.
Tarzan was a lonely man,
More than a snake, or a tree.
In self-reservation
He undertook
To keep it from himself.

Report about a Dream

I hover in the rounded space
of a washing-machine
or a vegetable scraper.
Its rough walls abrade my skin,
scarify my flesh.
Hovering in the revolving drum
I realize it is the world.

I note that it is
A hostile, alien world.
Here and there I see
scraps of sheepskin
on the grater walls.
Friends they are, I think,
astonishing myself with the conclusion.
And reassured, almost serene, I wake.

A couple of weeks later I sat in front of Ezra Sussman, whose slender body moved rhythmically as he tried to find the scansion in my verse. (I watched him anxiously: I didn't know what it was he was looking for, and whether or not it was there.) My heart swelled when he asked the tea lady passing in the corridor of the fourth floor of the *Davar* building to bring his visitor, too, a glass of yellowish tea. Under the desk his slim low-cut shoes contrasted with the coarse appearance of my work boots, but I regretted having such prosaic thoughts at such a moment. On the midday bus going back to the kibbutz I thought it was foolish of me to imagine that I was stuffed with layers which were not me, because my problem wasn't that I was too much like others, but that I was not sufficiently like them.

As we left Tel Aviv, the bus window cleared and the palm trees leading to Mikveh Israel seemed bigger and greener than ever, as though I was seeing them through a magnifying glass. The pane kept growing clearer, and for a moment I felt that the choice was mine. Though the words I'd grown up with were unrelated to my fears and the smell of my loneliness, I had learned to place some of them as landmarks, and to demarcate a territory of my own. Sometimes I was able to strike them together, like flints, and produce sounds of my own. When we were in sixth grade I saw Batsheva hiding something in the heap of dirty clothes in the corner of our shower room. I could not control my curiosity and discovered a big, round bloodstain on her white panties. I froze at the sight. The blood in my chest stopped flowing and thumped heavily in my ears. A fateful verdict, which I wanted to put off forever, was carrying Batsheva and the other girls to unknown regions. Now, sitting on the bus, I knew that this time I was the departing one, and at last the loneliness was not a weakness, not a plea. The orange groves on the road to Rishon Letziyon glowed through the magnifying lens of the bus window, and on the west shone the light fields of the seashore. A passenger sitting behind me asked, in broken Hebrew, how to get to Ramlah. When I replied my voice came from a lower place in my throat, as if I'd only just discovered the right source of speech.

Three years earlier, at the end of Independence Day celebrations, there were fireworks on the main lawn, for the first time in the history of the kibbutz. For a moment I looked up, thrilled, at the blue, green, and purple canopies that spread open above us, dripped their lights quickly and dissolved in the night sky. Then I hung my head, choking, intimidated, uncomprehending. The crushed grass was strewn with plastic cups, empty soft-drink bottles, and smeared paper napkins. Cries of admiration went on over my head, and I couldn't understand why I couldn't join my voice to theirs and point with the hundreds who stood on the lawn at the dawn colors which repeatedly blazed and went out in the darkness. Now as the passengers swung back and forth in unison when the bus stopped at the entrance to the main depot in Rishon Letziyon and in Ness Tziyona, my body swung with them, pacified and calm as that of a pregnant woman.

III

COMPLETIONS

The Return Home

Tuesday afternoon. Many of our classmates—Dinah's, Elan's, and mine—came to sit with us at Mom's place after the funeral, and so did Mom's erstwhile nursing charges. The flight, the funeral, and the renewed encounter with the kibbutz had tired me out. I sat at the table in silence. Despite my tiredness I discovered that I wasn't dazed; on the contrary, my mind was perfectly clear. Without looking out, I knew that the winter sun was just then going down over the distant citrus grove, and how in a few moments night, damp, thick, and cold would descend on the kibbutz, and darkness would swallow up the tall palm tree avenue north of Herzl Forest and the cypresses fringing the cemetery. I knew all the visitors by name, as well as the names of their parents and siblings, and knew as well—as though it permeated through my skin—the degree of warmth with which each one uttered words of comfort and consolation. Quite naturally, as though it were a sense or an instinct, I absorbed all the hints and signals that trailed the spoken words, and knew what was filtered out of them. As I looked across the room, the expressions and lip movements of the ones I couldn't hear were transparent as glass: I knew exactly which smile had an inner smile behind it, and which was ingratiating or hid an old grievance.

Equally transparent was the self-consciousness I remembered so well from my childhood: the constant awareness of how one is perceived, how one is judged by the others. As if the kibbutz had created a language of its own, in which every word was addressed not only to the hearer, but also to a potential audience. With what enthusiasm we danced in the dining hall at festivals and weddings, proud of the sweat that glistened on our brows, relishing the movements of the dance and our supple, young bodies, while at the same time putting on a show, acting our roles ("Kibbutz youngsters expressing the joy of the holiday in dance"; "Kibbutzniks dancing with youthful naturalness") before ourselves and before the older kibbutz members watching us from their chairs around the walls.

And the same familiarity revealed to me the greedy materialism in the eyes of our visitors: how much did that jean jacket cost and those leather shoes, and where did you buy them, and how much did the Toyota Corolla cost, whose keys are in the bunch on the table. (The sharp transition from Gainesville to Hulda revealed to me that this materialism went hand in hand with our inveterate gossip mongering, but I was too tired to figure out the nature of the connection.) We had always known, from our earliest days, that we were princes—penniless princes, but blue-blooded for all that. Then, when the sense of nobility expired, it was necessary to start everything from scratch, without a profession and without assistance from the family. Once there was an ideology of poverty—simplicity, modesty, the voluntary renunciation of private property. But when the ideological rug was pulled out from under us, only coarse materialism remained, the materialism of poor people who perceive the things of the world not in terms of their usefulness, their nature or beauty, but in terms of their price tag. (Curiously enough, contemporary Hebrew literature lacks all reference to material problems. Glancing mentally over the bookshelves in my house in Evven-Yehuda and in Florida, I could not recall a single fictional character who is seriously worried about "finishing the month" without enlarging the overdraft, or about the retirement pension, or the need to help the children buy an apartment of their own. It would be interesting at some time to try and work out why Hebrew literature ignores such a central factor in its readers' world.)

This familiarity with the people around me—the complete familiarity which is primarily with oneself—brought a tremendous sense of relief. Only a few days before I had chaired a meeting of the department at the university, and I now realized how opaque my colleagues' faces were to me, seen always on the surface, their expressions and comments requiring interpretation and never grasped with complete certainty. Sitting at my mother's table I didn't have to make an effort: people smiled at me, patted me on the back, accepted me the way members of a family accept one another. I sat there in silence, feeling something inside me thawing and melting into a thick, vocal togetherness, whose seductive pleasure I had long forgotten. In the seventies I used to swim in the sea all year round, attempting to shake off my tendency to catch colds (Mom described to me many times how she carried me in her arms all the way from Ekron to Hulda after the *brith* that was done at the hospital—to which I always responded with the comment, Sure, and I've had a cold ever since). On very cold days I went to the Gordon Swimming Pool in Tel Aviv. It is outdoors, but I could take a hot shower after the swim. Standing shivering under the streaming hot water, I used to think, I can't imagine why, "Warmth is God." Now again, in the crowded room, I felt myself absorbed into the warmth, and "How sweet it is when brethren sit together." (I've noticed that we don't keep the same physical distance from each other as Americans do—we stand close together, rubbing against each other without discomfort. Over there, slices of tomato and cucumber are laid separately on the plate, unmixed, unseasoned. Here an Israeli salad, chopped fine and drenched with dressing, is dumped amid the other dishes in the army mess tin.) "Oh how sweet it is," someone inside me warbled, "when brethren sit together."

I had traveled far to institutionalize my loneliness. Much effort had gone into bolstering my solitary pride, the pride of the impoverished. (Always alone, pulling myself strenuously out of the water, holding myself up by my suspenders, while behind the careful smile lurks a childish hunger for contact.) In the mid-eighties I was offered an assistant professorship at the University of Michigan. In my first years at Ann Arbor (where the sky exposes its blue color no more than fifty days in the year) my social life consisted of a weekly meeting with one or another colleague. I used to think all week about the forthcoming meeting as a kind of medicine, a pill of concentrated socializing to help me keep my sanity. How could I have forgotten the sweetness of being brethren together. How could I have forgotten the togetherness that is moist and warm and flowing, that here we are beautiful and confident and in the right, illuminating one another with that old princely light. In our high-school years we used to hang around on Friday nights after supper on the balcony of the children's house, the gang talking and laughing and making plans for that evening or the next day, and for a few moments, by an unplanned process that one hoped would recur, there was a warm, hugging togetherness. How could I have forgotten. Avigdora passed her hand over my skinny arm and stated, "My, you've really gained some weight in the last thirty years," and we both laughed, a deep belly laugh, totally unrelated to her comment, a laugh that could only arise from untold years of complete, skin to skin, familiarity. I had to kill my father for it, but I was home.

Early Days

Wednesday, the second day of the shivah. It's almost noon, and a winter stillness hangs over the kibbutz, the stillness of the lawns and the bare trees. The wind carries the subtle smell of the rotting heaps of pecan leaves. How shrunken it all is. A mere few yards from my parents' place to the dining hall, and about the same distance from the dining hall to the kibbutz yard. Then no more than two hundred paces to the gate. A small community, entirely enclosed within its boundaries. It begins here, at the rusting sheepfold sheds near the road, and ends there, past the last of the veteran members' houses. No dangling bits, no margins, no straggling houses along the highway to tell travelers that they're approaching a human settlement. No wonder that as children we were so acutely aware that this place, within this fence, was ours, was "us," whereas anyone who came from outside—children who were sent to our local school, and spoke with a ridiculous accent, or groups of visitors who came for the festivals and walked around in pressed black trousers—were not "us," not ours. In those days the corrugated tin sheds of the smithy and the garage stood on one side of the road leading to the gate, and past them stood the concrete building of the joinery, the cowshed with iron railings around it, the silo pit and the sheep pen. On the other side of the road stood the cold-storage, the barn, the seed store, and the long henhouses (early in the morning the roosters vied with one another, their cock's crows rising in the air like their coxcombs, while the constant cackling of the thousands of chickens, on the other hand, flowed together into a dull rumble which you soon stopped hearing; you had to look at the henhouses to pick it up again). That was the order of the structures, as natural and inevitable as the order of the fingers or the alphabet, the musical scale, the gamut of colors and smells. It was such a pleasure to come back to it after the annual trips that took place at the end of every school year, or a short summer vacation at the house of my parents' friends in Kfar Hayim. It was exciting to catch the first sight of the water tower and the culture hall, and a few minutes later to walk among the familiar buildings and faces. Only here was the world known through and through, like the warm, moist palm of one's own hand, as familiar and proprietary as the underclothes that bear the smell of one's body.

The kibbutz yard is quite empty, but I can still see Hanoch walking down the road to the sheep pen, his body bent forward, not bowed but hurried. And Aharon Kornreich, husky as a prizefighter, marching to the cowshed, lifting his knees as though wading through water. Moshe Hess and Zvi Kasser—the former with his blue gaze pacing slowly like many tall men, and the latter, short and pudgy, hurrying behind with a puzzled air—are about to step off the road beyond the gate and take the dirt track leading to the olive grove. I can recall their footsteps, each with his innate walk, as distinct as handwriting. But what they all had in common was the grave expression, which assumed an air of humble diligence the moment it encountered another's gaze. They stared curiously at the few visitors who came here as though they were inanimate objects. The contemptuous humility in their eyes expressed their anxiety that the visitors might not recognize the grandeur of their enterprise.

The road in passes between the abandoned sheep pens and henhouses and across the bare concrete of the cowsheds. Visitors are asked to park their cars in the kibbutz parking lot, before the road turns towards the dining hall. Now, in broad daylight, I realize that this parking lot, where stands our white Peugeot, is exactly where my first home used to be. A row of wooden huts emerges from the mists of my memory. Mine was the third room in the second hut. When I close my eyes momentarily, the mist dissolves somewhat and reveals black insulating material lining the hut walls, a strip of pavement, a palm tree, and a temporary bathroom. The gray tiles of the porch sink into the ground; through the murky glass of the years the dirt quickly rises between them. Grass grows wild beside the hut, with brown ants marching up and down its blades, as though to measure their height. The leaves of the burdock that squirms between our hut and the next are as rough as a calf's tongue. Behind the house are eucalyptus trees, and Elan climbs on them and frightens me from among the branches with a broken black doll. Inside the house is a big bed, an oblong table, and four backless chairs. A house. An ordinary house. My arms and body amaze me with a memory of skin rubbing, hugging: when you hang the bedspread over the gap between the table and the bed a dark cave appears in the room. Inside the cave a little boy flounders, twists, turns from side to side, a butterfly trying to become a cocoon once more. It is so much safer, stronger, embraced, so much more complete to be and not be in this darkness. In the evenings the black earth of the fields rises to the height of the electric pole opposite, but inside the house glows a pleasant, yolk-like light. A few pictures flash from the deep mist: Father lifts me up with one hand, high as high can be, before a row of people standing beside our hut. The people below me grin and laugh, and I can't understand how they fail to see that I'm about to break my neck falling from this awful height. Or: Elan and I each get a brown cookie every evening (while the packet, brought by Father's sister from Tel Aviv, lasts). Elan has not yet come from his children's house, and I can't resist it—I bite the ear of his cookie. His bitten cookie is lying solitary in the big tin, and I'm unable to bear my own iniquity. I stand in the corner, sobbing: "Tell him a mouse ate it!" (To whom did I make this appeal? I see myself shrinking in the corner, but can't see who is bending over me.) What did the four of us do in the evenings in that small room? I can remember nothing. I hang around awhile longer, but memory doesn't answer the knock on its door. Only the sense that with Father it's best to be beside him, and with Mom in front. Her big body relents a little when you lean against it, it softens, makes room for a cheek, for an eye. Memory, which seemed worn as a pebble in the stream, suddenly pierces me like a needle.

By the time I returned to my parents' place the visitors had all left. Some kibbutz women, with kind memories of their childhood nurse, have brought various cooked dishes, and we don't need to prepare anything for lunch.

"Mom, what did we use to do together in the hut in the evenings?"

"Faigele mine, you still remember the hut? You were two, three years old. What do you mean, what did we do? What every family does. Whatever it was, we were happy," she pleads. "You know what we had in that hut?" she asks my wife. "For a table we used two suitcases, one on top of the other, and for chairs we used four empty jerricans of olives, which I

covered with embroidered cloths." Two suitcases, one on top of the other?
Olive jerricans? I remember a table and chairs. My mind is too weary to
rework this new information.

In the evening the place is crowded again. Elan, Dinah, and I are enjoy-
ing being together and seeing old classmates, who come from all over the
country to condole with us, so the weight of the bereavement falls mainly
on Mom. By ten-thirty everyone has left. Elan goes outside to smoke,
Dinah is washing up, and Mom turns to me and picks up where we left
off: "What did we use to do? Well, we didn't spend much time together
in the hut. Father used to come home at six and I at seven. By the time
we rested a bit and changed our clothes, it was time to take you to the
children's house and put you to bed." She is sitting in the chair Father
used to occupy in recent years, propping her head on her hand, just as he
used to do. But unlike him, she doesn't doze off. "I was a children's
nurse," she tells my wife, "and didn't get home till seven, can you imagine?" she flutters her hand hopelessly. Her tear ducts are as big as her eyes.
Suddenly I understand why I can recall with such clarity the threads of
dirt between the tiles in front of the hut. "In the spring, after the lambing,
we used to keep the newborn lambs in a separate pen. We only let them
through after the evening milking, and then there was such a rush!" Mom
concludes on a high, astonished note that hangs in the air. My wife and I
exchange puzzled looks. "You loved to watch it, don't you remember?"
Mom says to me, to overcome the silence. A current of emotion which
could turn into either a cry or a smile, like underground water seeking an
outlet, emerges as a smile. It begins on her lips and ends on mine. No one
can take this cry away from us.

Birth

Thursday. Before retiring to my siesta, I switch on the television. There are few programs, but one of them, a BBC nature program about cheetahs, has me rooted to the spot. The cheetah is hungry, and its food has just been thrown into the world. In a few moments I see one of the most moving scenes I've ever seen on the small screen. Or perhaps it's the extra sensitivity I've been prey to since the funeral.

Birth

> The program about the cheetahs
> opens with a doe giving birth.
> The moist fawn struggles to stand up, topples, staggers
> on matchstick legs, presses against its mother,
> seeking her teats.
> The doe pushes it away
> (to accustom it to standing on its legs, the voice says).
> From afar, with yellow slitted eyes,
> a cheetah watches her prey.
> Crouching, soundless, she advances.
> The fawn's young life flees,
> swerving aside with unexpected skill.
> But the cheetah closes in.
> She smacks it with her paw.
> It flies, lands with a thump,
> then, dazed and shocked,
> it rises once again.

The cheetah, accustomed to fast, fleeing food,
stands by, panting.
Watchful, she puts her paw on it
as though in play.
This fawn, with innocent child's face,
this tender fawn (three kilos in the great scheme of life)
looks up at the big warm body,
raising its muzzle, open-mouthed,
to the teats that should be there, overhead,
in the warm enfolding
hairy breathing bosom.

[That fawn,
the little know-nothing,
nuzzles the cheetah
(as though the chase was a mistake,
a misunderstanding
that must be overlooked),
seeking the teats that surely must be there
somewhere in the warm, hairy belly
overhead.]

What Have They Done to You?

Dunya, Mom asks her sister, should I have my picture taken with or without the hair band? She pulls out of her wardrobe winter coats, blouses, chucks them on the bed, tries hats and scarves in front of the heavy mirror. My right side is best, isn't it? she says and answers herself. A young woman, confident of her beauty, she knows the exact tilt of the head for the photograph, knows that hair and features are only the foundation, the base on which there may be changes and additions which won't alter the color of the eyes, but can show clearly how beautiful life is and full of promise, because the future holds so many possibilities, and all of life is still ahead of her—the only question is, from what angle to peep at it, with what smile to charm it. Then she obeys the photographer's instruction and smiles back. Her dresses and coats, her parents' home, her five brothers and sisters, and her father's oil factory, they all swaddle her as cotton swaddles the citron for Tabernacles. Look at me, says the photographer at Zimmerfeld's photographic studio on Bricheva's main street. But she looks beyond him, to the future that lie ahead, that beckons and promises. Every afternoon for the past five years she has attended meetings of the Gordonia movement in her town, and goes home in the evening. For five years she has been hearing stories about the early kibbutzim, about the simple, communal life in Eretz Israel, and her heart longs to be there, with Shaindel and Sima and David Haimowitz, and the score of comrades who have already made the journey and established the movement's first kibbutz.

Ten o'clock. In the adjoining room (once a porch which was enclosed and made into a kind of sitting room) are the last visitors. There will probably be no more callers tonight, the third night of the shivah. Mom tells Yaffa and Zvi, old comrades from the "Bessarabian group," about Father's last hours. Amazing how quickly she has adopted the formula "Yonah, rest his soul," or "Father, rest his soul." I am in the bedroom, looking through the family photos in the decorative wooden box. I know that most of their relatives are here, but I don't recognize any of them. How well I remember this box and the sense of remoteness the photos evoked to me as a child, these rounded faces in black and white in their alien diaspora world. Some of the photos bear dates and names in hesitant Hebrew letters. And here is Mom. The richness of the Bessarabian landscape looks out of these three photographs of her, taken in 1935, when she was twenty. This is an unknown Mom, Mom who takes care of her appearance and enjoys it. I can just hear her turning gaily to her younger sisters, asking: What do you think, Dunya, with or without a hair ornament? Or: Sarahlé, do you mind if I borrow your colorful scarf for the picture? This is Mom entering life, her big eyes filmed over with a dream, like the silk paper protecting engravings in a book. Out of a clutch of photos in my hand drops another picture of her, taken almost thirty years later, and my heart sinks. I'd like to stretch out my hand to her, to stroke her thinning hair. Just look what they have done to you, not only the three decades but the kibbutz, too—as if the destruction of feminine beauty has always been one of the goals of revolutions.

This is the Mom I know well: her dry, freckled skin, exposed to the sun and the wind, has always been our family escutcheon. In the early photos, her eyes dominate, aware of their size and open not only to the photographer, but to the fullness of the life waiting outside. In the late picture they gaze soberly at the photographer, asking if he's finished and when the pic-

ture will be ready. She's looking straight at the lens, no longer thinking about the best angle, because it makes no difference. Thirty years in the kibbutz have drained the sap from her lips and crushed their smile. That confident, mysterious smile faded on the soil of the kibbutz, vanished among the walls of the children's houses. The thin lips, like a poorly watered furrow, are pressed tight to avoid uttering aloud what the heart already knows.

She cut off her long black hair, which she used to draw back with a band or cover with a smart hat, as soon as she came to the kibbutz. Ever since then she has worn it short, brushed back, easily combed with her fingers. And if a strand should come loose, so what? One is not judged by one's appearance but by the quality of one's work. Mom is a children's nurse who comes home after dark, and she's always tired, always exhausted. The hairstyle in the late picture is a minimal one, something done out of necessity, not a thing that a woman may enjoy, color, and change. And so is clothing in these parts—straightforward, avoiding all adornment or refinement. Like the food in the dining hall. We need to eat, so we eat, the same menu year after year, to gobble in fifteen minutes flat. You don't cut a piece of meat, then eat it—you cut it up in advance into a dozen small bits, as though this too is a job that must be done efficiently. Here what matters is the substance, as the kibbutz representative explains to visiting groups who come to observe the wonder of kibbutz life, not decorations or fiddle-faddle. And indeed everything is bare in this photograph: the face, the neck and the lips, and the bitter disillusion between mouth and eyes.

The ears are also bare, because the kibbutz person is a social one, a listening one—what are they saying about me, and who said it, and why isn't it possible to leave the room without always being talked about behind one's back. This social existence destroyed the feeling of self-value that colored the youthful portraits, eliminated the sense of distinction they radiated, the distinction of a girl whose family cherished her, her big eyes and her exquisite soprano, which made her presence mandatory in every party.

The heavy winter coats are absent in the late photograph on account of the sun, which blazes on the kibbutz most of the year and leaves no shadowy corners, but also because when she arrived Mom handed them over to the general clothing store. The coat with the fur collar disappeared in

Jerusalem the first winter after her arrival in the country. A kibbutz member wore it when she went to chilly Jerusalem to visit her relatives, and it never reappeared. Another woman member went to visit her relatives in Tel Aviv, taking them a jar of olives from the kibbutz grove. The jar left marks of caustic soda all over Mom's second coat, which ended its career. When Mom comes into the room to look for her glasses she tells me the story of her overcoats with a light, almost indifferent, laugh.

"What are you looking at so intently?" she asks, then sees the photos in front of me. "This was taken after the fair," she points to the photo from 1963. "I went to the fair, sold what I could, and went home. That's all," she concludes, never ceasing to amaze me.

She smoothes my hair with a tired hand and leaves me alone with the women she was sixty and thirty years ago. The future promises nothing, says fifty-year-old Mom to her young relative. I'm not complaining, she says with pursed lips, but it might have been better without all those dreams, without all that talk about a new society, a life of sharing and intimacy.

I call my wife to come and look at the photographs. She looks at them and at my face and I don't have to say a word. "I got my emotionalism from Mom," I say apologetically. "You're tired, come," she says. "Let's put you to bed." My mother's face follows me from her place to our temporary accommodation. The worn skin, the bitter disillusion, the silent sigh.

A Miss

Friday, the fourth day of the shivah. An extraordinary surprise: for the first time I hear the voice of my twenty-year-old mother, the girl with the dreams and the long hair. I'm not mad about the man she's in love with (though in the youthful photos he's a good-looking guy, and the title of emissary no doubt increased the charm of his shock of black hair), but in her native tongue she is a gay and witty girl, and her language expresses her love as the scent expresses the rose. This is not the serious woman with the short hair and impoverished Hebrew I have known all my life. Ten years before she walked with me for hours in the pouring rain, put me in the children's house, kissed me, and promised in an unaccustomed language to return and see me in the morning; her Yiddish is fluent and assured, capable of expressing precisely all the nuances of longing and loneliness. In ten years' time she will put me to bed in the children's house, on my first night in the kibbutz, and I shall lose her to the kibbutz and to Hebrew.

After lunch my mother called me to her bedroom and handed me a big brown envelope: the letters she and Father had exchanged during the four years between their meeting at the preparatory camp in Bessarabia and her arrival at the kibbutz in 1938. Father's letters, written closely in Yiddish on large sheets he tore out of a notebook, have all been kept, but only a few of Mom's letters survived. I found Hayim, an old member from the "Bessarabian group," in the Gordonia archive, where he was sorting documents. He glanced at his watch, hesitated briefly, then consented to translate a letter or two for me. I took one at random: Bendery, November 13, 1935. Like all my father's letters, it opened with the initials "H. Y." Hayim guesses that they stand for *Haverah Yekarah* ("Dear She-Comrade"). It appears that Mom's letters reached him every Wednesday. One week no letter arrived, and he was in agonies of anxiety for days. The letter before us was written two days later: "I can't fully express what a torment these days are to me, they are endless and weigh on my heart like a heavy, pressing burden. Even in the most cheerful moments, when people think I'm in a good mood and able to cheer up others, even then I am not happy. My heart trembles. It's as though my soul and my eyes are peering at the distance, searching for you, my girl. Only you can give me peace and genuine happiness. Only you can sooth and comfort my suffering heart, my stormy soul. Only you can bring me happiness in the purest sense of the word, happiness and strength to keep bearing the burden of life, the burden of the people and of the movement. My child, I can't believe that you would deliberately cause me such pain. Write to me, I beg you, don't keep me waiting." Hayim translated it carefully, started to say something (did he wonder, as I did, about my father bearing the burden of the nation and the movement on his shoulders?) but refrained. He held the letter up to his red, moist old eyes and shook it, as if to see if there were more words hidden among the lines. Then, like a tired child, he rested his furrowed, badly shaved cheek on his hand, and waited for my next request.

I found Mom's reply easily in the small batch of her letters. "Bricheva, November 25, 1935. Greetings to you, Balaban. How could you think for a moment that I deliberately delayed writing? Don't you know that your suffering is also mine? Oh my dear, who would have thought that we would have to sustain each other for so many weeks on mere pieces of paper." I asked Hayim to repeat the last sentence, and his heavy eyes stared at me, puzzled by my surprise. It was as though a window had opened and showed me that big-eyed young woman whose photographs I'd seen for the first time two days before. Did I then inherit my poetry from her Yiddish, which I had never heard? Hayim repeated the last few sentences, with the same intonation and the same dubious grimaces, then went on: "I am reading De Mann's book on the psychology of socialism. I read, and suddenly stop and begin to dream of different days, days which will not be filled with such longing, such loneliness. I see your whole form, my love. You are so vivid, that I feel you're beside me, and I try to call you to me. I call softly, so no one will hear. Every Saturday the post brings me a letter from you, but these past two Saturdays I waited in vain. I was left disappointed, alone in my silence. I could not sleep for entire nights. I lie on my bed and turn off the light. Then I turn it on again, because I'm unable to fall asleep. As soon as I shut my eyes I see you before me. I see your pale, sad face, and the sight stabs my heart. You cannot imagine my joy when I get your letter. Well then, goodbye. Write me at once."

Unbelievable: Mom and Father, like lovers since time immemorial, measuring their longings and suffering to each other. This great love surprises me. The atmosphere at home was always very matter-of-fact: two kibbutz members come home at the end of the day's work, drained of their strength, rest a little, read the newspaper, and get ready for supper or to put their children to bed in the children's houses. Both had grown up in homes where the husband was a rabbinical figure and the wife fussed around him, and the slogan of communal equality stopped at their doorstep. I never saw them stroke or hug each other, much less kiss. But the most stirring surprise, equal to that of her youthful photos, is the encounter with Mom expressing herself in Yiddish. When Father fell ill Mom took over the letter writing to me. Her Hebrew had remained poor and incorrect, confident only in expressing wishes of success, happiness, and good health. In her last letter, which reached me just before I flew to Israel, she reported the doings of Elan and Dinah, as usual, and concluded apologetically, "Excuse me, Avremalé, for all the misteaks. In my time there were no quick Hebrew corses and there was no way to learn it properly." The two closely written pages of her Yiddish letter showed me to what extent Hebrew diluted and distorted her personality. Compared with her awkward handwriting in Hebrew, in Yiddish her handwriting was assured and flowing, and her expression "as natural as breathing, like smelling a rose." Many sentences in it could have been translated directly into the passionate letters I'd written my wife only a few years ago, before we knew if we could join our lives, which had been proceeding along different routes.

For her, as for my father, Hebrew was a third or fourth language—after Yiddish, Russian, and Romanian. My father had been taught in Heder and knew some Hebrew from childhood. Mom acquired her Hebrew in the kitchen, in the clothing store and the cowshed. What was it like, to get up in the morning amid alien words, to go through the dining hall, the sounds of tent, of gravel, rota duties, baby and infant children's houses? Did Hebrew ever feel like home, an intimate space? For the past twelve years I've been dividing my time between the United States and Israel, and still a Hebrew page looks clear to me, while an English page looks opaque, requiring close, attentive reading. Whether speaking or writing, English to me is a bottleneck; it forces me to be content with the surface of things, it indicates distantly joy, pain, or laughter, never actually touches. I try to see the local paper through Mom's eyes: it looks like chunks of an alien, incomprehensible language.

Hayim caught my curiosity and agreed to translate one more letter. "Bricheva, December 4, 1935. Greetings to you, Balaban. Your letter arrived only today. I didn't know what to think. These past days robbed me of so much resistance and strength. And today's letter is not too happy either. In your last letter you wrote that your arm was well again, yet in this one you say that it's better and you're able to move it a bit. So it hasn't really recovered. Why did you keep it from me?

"You asked me to send you 2500 lei to take of the immigration papers. I'll send them tomorrow, maybe today if there's time. I'll send 4000 lei, so you'll have enough to buy material for a suit and pay the dressmaker. I told my father that you need 3500 lei for the papers and 500 for Bucharest. He didn't object, so get yourself a suit and I'll be very pleased. You see, I've become a bit of a liar in my old age.

"Yesterday I almost went to Belz. Something broke in the oil-making machinery at the factory, and my father doesn't travel on the Sabbath. In the end I didn't go, because of the cold. When you were here the place was a quagmire, and now the mud is frozen. It's fabulous—positively a second Paris." Hayim laughs: "You can't imagine the mud. Before it froze you practically had to go down on all fours to cross the street." He adjusted the reading lamp and resumed reading. I listened to him with my eyes shut. I'm meeting my mother for the first time, half a century after she brought me here. Her hair is long, the skin taut on her prominent cheekbones; she is sitting at the massive table in her room, writing a letter. Her longing and loneliness cannot obscure her independence and the confidence with which she conducts her affairs, the confidence of a girl who has been nurtured with love in a prosperous home. In her mother tongue, in her mother's home, she chats with youthful fluency, wit, and humor—so unlike the woman I'm familiar with, whose speech is hesitant, who struggles for the right word and glances sideways to see what others think of what she's saying.

Hayim apologized, saying he had to leave (should I offer to pay him? For a moment I mixed up times and places), and offered a similar meeting next week, if I wished. The kibbutz is taking its siesta and I go for my daily walk. "Who would have thought that we would have to sustain each other for so many weeks on mere pieces of paper." Who would have thought that Mom wrote this?

Opposite the cemetery, where once was the olive grove, there is now a broad field of melons. I strolled down the limestone path separating the long rows of melons from the cemetery, and returned to the kibbutz courtyard. Once when I was a kindergarten child playing on the big lawn on a Saturday afternoon, I heard the grown-ups say they were off to pick melons. It was the first year that melons were cultivated in the kibbutz, and the members were looking forward to the first fruits. I wanted to bring Mom a surprise gift of melons, but didn't know what they looked like. The word "melons" sounded like "millions," and I visualized them as a mass of little greenish olives and wondered how they would be carried home. The wide field near the orange grove was covered with rows of rusty green leaves. Then one of the members showed me what melons were, and suddenly the rough leaves were filled with orangey-yellow fruits, and the word "melon," so round and smooth, became inseparable from the fruit itself.

That summer the children in the kindergarten next to mine had a tortoise they had found in a nearby field. One day I secretly removed the little creature, whose mushroom-brown shell had not yet hardened, and laid it in a box I'd prepared for it near the joinery. A moment later the tortoise poked its triangular head out of its hidey-hole and began to nibble the wilting lettuce in the box. Now I have a tortoise of my own, I thought gleefully, but as I walked uphill from the joinery to the children's house, the little reptile's nibbles gnawed inside me. I examined myself in the terms I knew: Am I afraid to be caught? Am I afraid they'll know I stole it? None of them quite fitted the case, but the gnawing did not stop, and before I got very far I knew for a fact that it would ruin my pleasure. I turned around and I took the tortoise back to its owners. In years to come I'd find the word that would fit that gap, and identify with it. A second language would bump into a blocked, occupied space, and would grow slowly on a side of the brain, pale as a plant grown in a cellar. After all these years in the United States, Hebrew retains its immediacy, like vision and hearing, like an instinct, while my perception in English is delayed, translated. As I went on walking towards the old access road of the kib- butz, the cowshed and sheep pen and the eucalyptus outside the gate, I could readily find English words for the sights around me, but the images raised by the English words were abstract and blurry, like pallid illustra- tions in a textbook. What scent, color, root, and foliage did the English "eucalyptus" have, compared to the patient, swamp-draining power of its Hebrew pronunciation? A few days earlier I'd phoned the office of one of the university deans, and asked to speak to the secretary Michelle. "Michelle? There's no one here by that name," a woman's voice replied with a chuckle. I apologized and hung up. I checked my papers and found that the secretary I was looking for was named Leslie. I called again and asked for Leslie—she was the person who had answered my earlier call. How could I explain that in my mind the names Michelle and Leslie occu- pied the same pigeonhole (a female name that was an empty label, while being somewhat unusual, exotic), which would not have happened to me with Hebrew names such as Talli, Lili, or Gilli.

In the kibbutz courtyard the smell of cow dung mixed with the sour odor of hay. A cow lowed—a penetrating, moist sound, far-reaching as the hoot of a departing ship. How to describe the intimacy I feel in this courtyard, on the broken, muddy road that leads from the cowshed and seed store to the sheep pen (abandoned now, as though it had been des- tined from the start to serve as an infrastructure for cobwebs) and the gate? Perhaps like the intimacy of a chewed bit of food that a sudden cough ejects from the mouth. Or the intimacy one feels about one's dirty underwear. For better or worse, my world. Skies and cirrus clouds, black soil sticking to the shoes, damp ground and silvery-green weeds that in a month or two will reveal their prickly nature, the lowing of cows and bleating of sheep—no longer heard—and in the distance—pastures, wheat fields, meadows, and furrows: words that cling to my mind like a clod of earth around a root.

And Mom? We imagined that we were living in the same world, the same dining hall, the same children's houses, we thought we were speak- ing the same language when we walked on the muddy paths in winter. Her mother tongue and my mother tongue (Hebrew was indeed anything but my mother's tongue) walked on these paths like strangers on railroad plat- forms, searching for the lighted signs, pushing and being pushed, passing each other in haste.

Laboratory Child, Laboratory Mother

Saturday, three o'clock in the afternoon. The first visitors will be here in an hour or two, and in the meantime Mom goes about turning out old drawers, opening yellowing cardboard files, trying to interest me in old writings of Father's, some in his handwriting—comic sketches for festival celebrations and meticulous reports on the apple harvests. "Does this interest you?" she asked, offering me a brown cardboard folder in which she had kept booklets from courses for children's nurses and articles on education in our local newspaper.

I am most interested in the old kibbutz newspapers from the years before I was born. Proposals for improving the social situation, plans for increasing the number of dairy cows and expanding the sheepfold, proud reports on the olive and apple harvests, and on the same page, one after the other, reports on the number of children who started first grade and the number of chicks transferred from the incubator to the henhouse. And here are the articles of Ozer Huldai, the school principal, because of which these papers were kept. The cheap, crumbling paper holds the matrix according to which my life was managed, unbeknownst to me. I read these texts with an embarrassed grin, like a laboratory child who has inadvertently come across the plans of his experiment.

IN THE COMMUNITY *(the local paper), August 15, 1941*
ON THE SUBJECT OF SCHOOL IN THE COMMUNITY
In my opinion we must do our best to adapt the conditions of the child's life, as early as possible, to our goals, so as to make it easier for him to adjust to the needs of the community, and to inculcate the values whose adoption has taken us a difficult internal struggle.

I have not yet formed a definite opinion about all the problems of bringing up children in the community. I cannot offer an unequivocal view, and I therefore demand that the community let me start with the most appropriate experiment. It would be a trial year for the community, in which the members will study the problem together with me. I have several questions in mind, but I cannot start categorically, although my ideas seem to me sound, until I have acquired at least one year's experience of working with children.

This is how I see the scheme of a day's work with the schoolchildren:

6 o'clock—rising, bathing, exercises
7 "—working, garden, etc.
8 "—breakfast
8:30 "—educational work, individual and group
10 "—recess
10:30 "—concentrated study, reading aloud, etc.
12 "—lunch
12:30 "—rest
1:30 "—Bible and Aggadah
2:30 "—Free time
5:30 "—Summary discussion
6:45 "—Supper
7:15 "—Parents
8:15 "—Bedtime

PARENTS AND WORKERS

It is in the child's interest to bring about a minimal understanding between these two main elements affecting his life. If such an understanding is impossible, there must at any rate be no interference between the two. If it is agreed that the child must not be in the adults' dining hall, the parents must not encourage a violation of this rule. It does not show the child an exceptional love, but lack of discipline in the parents themselves—and who can foresee the consequences.

Perhaps we can agree on some basic rules:

- Parents do not enter the children's houses, even if they hear their child crying and screaming;
- Parents do not enter the children's houses to chastise them;

- Parents do not promise their children anything that calls for advance consultation with the educators, until after such a consultation;
- The educator does not act as the parents' aid in imposing their direct discipline on their children;
- An agreement between the children and the educator in a given matter must under no circumstances be broken.

O. H.

The writer's affectedly modest aggressiveness matches the slim figure I remember walking briskly through the kibbutz, emanating a chilly superiority. Here everything is structured, organized. The educators are rearing natural children, sturdy as oak trees, passing them ceremoniously from the baby group to the infant group, from the infant group to nursery school, kindergarten, and first grade. The members listen attentively to the lectures of Ozer Huldai at the general members' meetings and the education committee, forbidding their hearts to reveal to their mouths that at night the thin reeds of fear add up to a thick sheaf, unable to see their children's striped pajamas gleaming in the dark on the paths and on the roofs, walking on air with the confidence of angels.

Working in the kibbutz plantations and vineyards, my father and his comrades cultivated apples, olives, and pears, molding their canopies as instructed by the agricultural specialists. The school principal applied the same methods to their children—powerfully imposing his authority and his bile on the members—and the tender shoots, those stubborn saplings that didn't know what's good for them, kept breaking out of their boundaries time again, making him a frustrated and bitter man. But only when I read the next paper did I understand why he proposed to send the children to their parents for a single hour a day, even when the cumulative experience of older kibbutzim had worked out a schedule that enabled the children to spend the afternoon and evening at their parents' house.

AUGUST 7, 1942
PROBLEMS

In my opinion, those who think that the communal education weakens the bond between parents and children and reduces the parents' influence, are mistaken. On the contrary, I permit myself to assert that there is no other way of life in which the bonds between children and parents are as powerful as in the commune. There is no other way of life in which the influence of parents upon children is as marked, as active, directing and forming the child's personality, as it is in the commune, in the communal education. The greater the communal element in education, the stronger the links between the parents and the children in their respective groups.

What is the situation in other ways of life that we know? The child spends several hours a day in kindergarten or school, and the rest of his time with his friends or at home. He has a particular relationship with his family, one that allows him to know his family, and such knowledge is by no means always positive; it may also imply conflicts, dissatisfaction, and profound disappointments. The child views his parents through his own eyes, unbiased and uninfluenced by other factors. He may also develop a critical attitude to his parents without fear of creating complexes in himself, without fear of being unduly suppressed by his environment. He does not have to be always on guard to defend his parents.

In the commune a child is always in the company of other children; he lives his entire life with them. The children know his parents, and he knows theirs. His knowledge is based not only on his own experience, but also on the experience of his parents and of various other members of the commune. The child absorbs impressions, opinions, not only about other members, but also about his parents.

He has no opportunity to form his own opinion about his parents— the community and the children's society pressure and compel him to consider their views. The possibilities of criticism all around are such, that there is absolutely no room for him to form his own criticism. He therefore develops a stubborn self-defense, a defense of what is his own, of his parents, without any objective observation whatsoever.

Outside the commune, if Fatherdy is a sergeant, the child can be quietly proud of the fact, while also viewing the father objectively. But in the commune, if Fatherdy is a sergeant, he rules over the others, he commands the parents of other children; the child is proud and shows off, voicing this feeling to his comrades, and surely every child wants his father to have something that he can be proud of. Outside the commune, Sergeant Fatherdy sometimes chastises him during the day. Outside the commune, the child occasionally bothers Sergeant Fatherdy and pays the penalty. In the commune, however, he sees Sergeant Fatherdy only when he is free, when he is able to spend his leisure with his son, to lend him his cap and his belt and go for a walk with him.

Outside the kibbutz, if Fatherdy is responsible for security, the child does not even know about it, or has only a vague idea. In the commune, however, in such a case the entire community is under his command, he is all-powerful and all the children are aware of it. The same may be said for every role, for every occupation. The need to find something in my father of which I may be proud, something that would enable me to defend myself and my family's prestige, is so great that sometimes children get carried away with fantasies about their fathers, and imagination steps in to fill the gaps in reality.

Add to this the fact that in the commune the child enjoys his time with his parents, because they do everything to make him feel happy in their company—because in that time it is forbidden to chastise a child even if he transgressed, because it is only one hour and the child must not be distressed, because it is just before bedtime, and it is known that a child must not be upset before going to sleep—and what you get is perfection.

OZER HULDAI

I'm stunned: this man with his twisted mind dominated the local educational system for decades. I ask Mom to read the article. She sits beside me, her hands on her knees, like an obedient child, and reads quietly, her lips moving. Then she looks up to me, as to a teacher. It appears that she is very good at text comprehension. She does not need to reread it to realize that the statements about the great importance of parenthood in the commune are totally contradicted by the measly, decorative role the writer actually assigns to parents. Half a century late, she is amazed to discover that the greatness of the communal educational system lay in preventing its pupils from seeing their parents objectively. Only in the commune, so says her school principal, does the child form his parents' image in accordance with social pressure, aided by his creative imagination which fills in the missing reality. "Why was it so important to him that the children shouldn't see us objectively?" she wonders, suppressing her bitterness, aware that it is too late to get mad.

Hulda, 1942. The first members settled in Herzl Forest nearly ten years ago, and three years ago the commune formally celebrated the move to a new settlement, one kilometer north of the forest. The young commune has few stone houses: the sunlight gleams on the row of children's houses, lined up north to south, and facing them, the homes of the kibbutz members. Beyond the children's houses rises the massive structure of the dining hall. On its other side, on the slope leading to the courtyard, stands a row of wooden huts. At the end of the day, having sent her kindergarten children to their parents, Shprintza goes to her room in a hut. There she finds her husband and her two-year-old son Elan waiting for her. She is tired after a long day's work, but not too much to enjoy being with her son. When he was nine months old, the nurse left him in a playpen on the porch on a cold winter day, and the glands in his throat swelled. At the general meeting the nurse asked to remove him from the children's house, to avoid infecting the other children. At that time Shprintza and her husband had not yet moved into a hut, and the tent in which they lived was unsuitable for a sick child. Another couple offered to keep the baby in their room till he recovered. Now, in 1942, Elan is two years old, and has only a small scar at the base of his throat to show where he was operated on. His mother is happy that she can see him every evening in her room. She changes her work clothes, then takes her son to the children's house. The lullabies she sings him blend with the stories and chatter around the other beds.

Hulda, summer 1942. I can imagine my mother reading Ozer Huldai's assurances, bravely and submissively. She has only been here four years and has picked up her Hebrew in the cowshed, the henhouse, and the children's houses. She doesn't know many of the words in the article. "When I got here he was already well known. He was the educated one, our intellectual," she says to me now, spreading her hands and letting them drop to her sides. Ozer Huldai is not around to prettify her image in my eyes: a woman of eighty-one, with the skin hanging in folds on her shrunken arms, like punctured balloons. Her whole strength lay in her belief, her innocence, her obedience and endurance. Now she has not the strength to bear the yoke of remorse. She echoes the phrases of encouragement and comfort that I say to her, trying to warm and fortify them in her mouth, and they remain hanging in midair, light and hollow.

Days of Crisis

Saturday evening. The living room was packed. I sat in the inner room and perused the folder Mom had given me after lunch. The papers which preserved the lofty ideas of Ozer Huldai also include editorials, which reveal that the period of grace enjoyed by the founding members did not last long. I sat on my father's bed and picked choice passages from the linguistic environment in which I grew up.

FROM THE EDITOR'S DESK, MAY 2, 1941
A TIME OF CRISIS

Times of crisis have become a part of our communal experience. Year after year, they recur as a necessary evil and become the hub of our lives. Everything revolves around this problem. Crisis in the committees, crisis in the posts, a social crisis. Communal life is always hard, but immeasurably harder at such times. What is the cause, wherein lies the root of this trouble? Some say, it's the sharpening of social relations; others think it's the general tension; undue obstinacy, is also a widespread belief. The majority think it's all of the above, and perhaps they're right. The conclusions are not far behind: resignations, strikes, conflicts, improper reactions, outbursts, pettiness, unwillingness to make concessions, lack of consideration for others—a tangled mass which poisons the air. Yet it is necessary to live, to work together, to maintain relations among us—but how to do it? How to emerge from the thicket and go forth on the highway? And the consequences are that people forget the boundaries, engage in personal attacks and irritable arguments, uncomradely responses (along the lines of: "So summon me before the committee!"), a heavy, burdensome atmosphere which sunders us apart.

It is mandatory to make a change, to correct things, but how?—Communally. Clear up detail after detail, explain, prove, persuade, and above all—solve. Not to ignore a mess without tackling it, without a clarification. Devote general discussions to the social predicament, investigate conflicts between the various industries and communal institutions, between members and officeholders, never leave any problems unresolved, never let things slide. This is a catastrophe; it embitters the life of the individual in questions, and then the entire community. Thoughtfully, without haste, patiently—otherwise we shall plunge into the abyss. The time of crisis has come—it must also pass, soon, and with cooperative goodwill.

STYLE—CONTENT—PURPOSE

These three are urgently needed, even more than economic recovery in these hard times. These can somehow be overcome. We can forgo some comforts—we have done so before, and at long last achieved economic stability. But that is not the case with the style of our life. Without it, it is hard to survive, and we cannot do without it. It must prevail among us. Of course, a style which is appropriate to our social aim. Especially when we recall that we are an independent community that lives with hardly any outside influence on our lives and internal organization. Like it or not, we are the models for ourselves and our children. We ourselves determine the style and we live by it. And herein lies the danger. That is why we must take care to maintain respectful relations among ourselves, so as to create an undistorted style of life to match our ideological education and cultural standard.

The absence of a healthy lifestyle is draining the meaning of our life as a commune. The positive side declines and the dominant content is quarrels, an unbridled venting of what must not be vented, a blurring of the boundaries between the permissible and the impermissible, improper sententiousness, social alienation, the individual in place of the community, a breakdown of understanding between people—the burning of bridges that lead to cooperative, productive, positive and efficient action. Where is the content? We must renew it. We must force ourselves to return to the right path. It is unthinkable that we should degrade our social value to a level of "Quarrel Company Inc." That was not the reason we chose to live together, to share the burden and, when necessary, to suffer. A constructive content in our life will sustain us through these stormy times. A different kind will destroy us. This is where purpose comes into it. There must be a purpose to the life of a substantial community in the special form of the commune. There must be purpose in cooperative action, cooperative struggle, and cooperative self-searching. Wherever we go, whatever we do, it is that which sustains our faith in our ultimate victory and the justice of our ideological and social assumptions. Had there not been a purpose to our efforts, our mighty enterprise would not have borne fruit. Man can do anything—build or destroy, affirm or deny, even risk his life and soul, only if there is a purpose to it.

In these past few weeks we seem to have somewhat forgotten this basic truth. We must be aware that we have distorted our own image and failed to take proper action to remedy it. Let us remember the style of our life, the content of our actions and the purpose of our existence.

ARYEH AVNON

The date of this piece, May 1941, surprised me. So the social hell began earlier than I had thought. Only a year or two previously, Hulda had moved, in a solemn ceremony, from the forest to its new abode. So here we are close to the beginning, to the mythical source.

The vocabulary and rhetoric of the article brought back the verbal world of my childhood, a world of discussion, debate and clarification, "reflections," "comments and insights." The mechanism was as simple and inescapable as a mathematical equation. There was a desperate need to find a solution, to adjust an everyday reality of quarrels and crises to a grandiose—yet hopeless—social ideal. There could be no real solution to these recurrent crises, because the kibbutz vision sought to create a new human being, free from desire for possessions and power—indeed, a human being whose only connection to the real individuals who created the kibbutz lay in wishful thinking. "One thing we didn't take into account," Hayim had said to me the day before, in his slow, old-man's rasp, interrupting his translation of Mom's letter. "Since we lived together we knew every person's failings. We knew that Mottalé didn't deposit all the money he'd brought from home in the kibbutz account, but put some of it aside. We knew that Baruch wasn't the most industrious worker, and if you didn't watch him he'd stop working, and that Sarka was a gossip always on the lookout for other people's faults, and that this person was such and that person was something else. But we thought that they were like that because of their background, and that it would be possible to explain things to them to discuss and to mend. What we didn't understand was that it wasn't just Mottalé and Sarka, but human nature. We were naive and idealistic," he nodded in disbelief. "We thought it was just a question of Mottalé."

As a result, words, clarifications, discussions, general debates, social committees, and articles in the local paper, all were recruited to tackle the situation. Since there was no hope of actually resolving the crisis, talking about it became a substitute solution, makeshift therapy. The kibbutz evolved a verbal culture in which language supposedly indicated the real conditions, but in fact existed in parallel to reality and detached from it, a language that dealt with the crises and their solutions while being itself the only remedy it could offer.

It was easy to see how the mechanism worked. The latter half of the article is devoted to the detailed description of what was lacking in the kibbutz, elements without which its life was not worth living. We do not have a suitable lifestyle, we have lost the content and purpose of our life. Yet this fact does not prevent the author from closing with a call to remember the style, the content, and purpose—as though these were actual facts, tangible and certain, which the members of the kibbutz had accidentally misplaced. The article throughout expresses wishful thinking ("We must take care to maintain respectful relations among ourselves"; "We must force ourselves to return to the right path"). Wish follows wish and need supports need: only a positive content can sustain the kibbutz, therefore the kibbutz must find the purpose of its existence. Finally, the writer forgets that he has been discussing wishes and needs, and concludes with the confidence of one who has hit on the right solution.

The particular status of language in relation to reality is shown in the very elements whose absence he bewails. The vague phrases (a "healthy lifestyle," a "constructive content") were close enough to certain elements in the readers' reality, and enabled the writer to disguise the fact that the only solution to the crisis was the discussion about it.

SEPTEMBER 26, 1941
ON THE CENTRAL PROBLEM—MAN IN SOCIETY
In the beginning was enthusiasm. For everything: the Zionist idea, the idea of realization, and above all, of cooperation. At that time Man was

willing to forgo his own self and his needs, sacrificing everything for the sake of creating a new society. A cooperative moment came into being, with settlements, enterprises, and tremendous achievements. Everything was dedicated to the field, the machine, and the livestock—almost nothing for man himself.

This period of enthusiasm could not continue forever. It dissipated very slowly, and we entered a period of realism. Now man said: "I was a good Zionist, a good socialist, but also a very bad man, because I failed to develop my own self; I became a spiritual and physical invalid. It is time to return to being a man." Man entered the period of realism with a massive burden of disappointment. It is well known that only a small step, a hairbreadth, separates enthusiasm from disappointment. This increased the danger. A time of crisis arrived.

Our hearts were drawn to the commune primarily because of the justice and equality it promised the individual. The encounter with reality exposed serious flaws. Classes appeared in the commune, as they did in the labor movement in general and the Eretz Israel one in particular. There are grievances in big and small matters. This feeling brings the individual to the edge of indifference. It leads to the collapse of the structure of faith in the basic values of the commune. Man is asking: "Who am I toiling for?"

I would say, "They could not see the forest for trees," or rather: "The might of the forest stopped us seeing the tree." Without the tree there is no forest, without the individual there would have been no cooperative movement. That is why *the man must be saved*, his value must be restored, he must be able to fully and freely express his individuality, regain his faith in communal society, be given what he needs, the air must be cleared, let man have his own corner to live in.

Nothing is too dear for this, because we must remember that the commune will stand or fall with the man, his weaknesses and gifts, his aspirations and emotions.

ARYEH AVNON

"Man" meaning the man in the commune. The member of the commune—not the child, and certainly not the "outside child," who was sent to the kibbutz for some reason. Aryeh Avnon was my class teacher from fifth to eighth grade. In my class there were thirteen kibbutz children and four or five "outside children." One of them, Benny, was the son of a wealthy family in Rehovot (it was at his birthday party, at his home, that

I first tasted avocado, and I can still remember encountering the buttery-green taste of the unfamiliar fruit. "They've got three toilets in the house!" we exclaimed, astonished, as we wandered about the spacious house). Purim parties in those days followed a regular pattern: all the school children stood in long rows in front of the kibbutz members, and each one stepped forward in turn and declaimed a line or two about his or her costume. These quips were composed by our teacher. That year Benny, who had difficulty pronouncing "s" and "sh," was dressed as an officer, and Aryeh composed a line for him to declaim that was stiff with S's and Sh's, and Benny writhed in discomfort, turned left and right, flung up his arms for succor, raised his eyes to heaven to avoid seeing the people in front of him, and naturally before he finished his declamation the entire kibbutz was rolling in the aisles, laughing. (Mention this incident to any of my classmates and you will hear the entire piece at top volume, with every dental sound fluffled to a turn.)

The article, however, is surprisingly frank. Years before Yizhar Smilansky described the spiritual miserliness of these world saviors and their offspring, Avnon provided an adequate description of their spiritual atrophy. Unlike previous articles, this one shows not only keen observation, but the ability to express a whole idea in a logical and consistent way. Nevertheless, he too cannot avoid the contradictions. How can a solution be found where there are none? Added to his wish list, which is supposed to save communal man ("his value must be restored, he must be able to fully and freely express his individuality . . . let man have his own corner to live in"), is the need to restore "his faith in communal society." But this was not an accidental loss that could easily be restored. That faith was damaged by the gulf between the communal vision and reality. How could it be restored, unless that gulf was essentially narrowed? Once more, we are in the realm of wishful thinking pretending to be solutions.

The pile of papers lies before me like the remains of an ancient, lost civilization. What a pity. What longings. Eons ago this was a human settlement. People rose early, put on blue work clothes, sowed and reaped, milked sheep and cows, mended plows. Morning, noon, and night they honed themselves to match the vision that had brought them to this place. Sometimes when eating a fresh orange and admiring the marvelous symmetry of its segments, they recalled digging the hollows (known as "saucers") for the trees and tending them patiently till the harvest, and this memory (arising all at once and too intricate to be fully grasped) prompted a sudden flush of joy that here they were, on the fertile, abundant ancestral land. In the spring everyone knew if the olive trees were bearing a good crop, and in the summer everyone took part in harvesting it (in groups, each spreading a carpet of sacks around a tree for the pebble-hard fruit to fall on, then excitedly counting the crates filled from the carpet), and a few months later everyone was sitting around the sorting tables and deftly sorting the olives, compulsively tasting now and then and urging themselves to stop. The eggs were ours, and the apples and the watermelons (such an aching longing to walk in sandals on the hot black soil through a watermelon field whose far end is shimmering in the summer vapor, punching open a ripe watermelon and devouring its dripping red heart), and we knew exactly how many thousands of liters our cows yielded per annum, and by how much the yield increased from year to year. The world was ours—not arbitrary, not bought at market price, but personal and familiar, trailing a long train of life, hopes, sweat, and laughs.

And a boy walked among the houses, talked to the birds, kicked a stone on the path, jumped up to touch an overhanging branch. Such a sorrow. I did not share all the joys of this place, but its dreams were my dreams. Those dreams had their times and occasions and meeting places; they had a singing image and a dancing image and the image of a column in the local paper, and the life that came after was dreamless, living on the broken fragments of dreams.

Dinah came into the room, wondering what I found so gripping in the old newspapers. On the front page of one of them she found the farewell song that used to be sung here at graduation from school:

> Radiant childhood, blessed years,
> Molten gold and pearl true,
> Mystery world, pure and clear—
> A farewell song we sing for you.

The lyrics were by Aryeh Avnon, and Aryeh Asa, the music teacher, poured into the melody the essence of nostalgic youth movement songs. Dinah stared at the familiar words as though suddenly encountering her lost childhood. I felt in my eyes the pressure of the nostalgia that made her eyes widen. She left the room, humming the song. The low hum was immediately picked up in the living room: some of the visitors joined her in low voices, self-consciously grinning, avoiding each other's eyes (I don't know why it called for personal intimacy, like the act of love. Or why, whenever I think about Aryeh Asa teaching us the youth movement songs in music lessons, one of the immediate associations that come to my mind is pornography). The song created an imaginary reality which bore no relationship whatsoever to our childhood, but for a moment that fictional childhood was the most tangible thing in the room. For a brief moment the visit of condolence turned into a soft requiem for a world that never was.

Portrait of Man as a Poet

"As a matter of fact, the land of our kibbutz was bought from the Arabs," Mom said to Hayim in an offended tone. She sounded unusually combative. I was not aware that she was following our conversation from the other side of the table. Hayim lowered his voice: "Put this question to your American students: you have discovered that your inheritance, which enabled you to buy a house for yourself and your family, originated from theft, from robbery. Say your father or grandfather were members of the mafia. Now, if you do the decent thing and return the property to its rightful owners, you and your family will be out on the street. All right, so you don't go that far, you want to hold on to your house, but surely you can admit the wrong, accept your responsibility, take an interest in the victims. You know what was the worst thing the kibbutz did to us? It made us indifferent. We learned to think only of ourselves, so now we stay at home like rats and do nothing, even when we know that around the corner, or a couple of miles away, a dreadful injustice is being committed."

During the early seventies we both taught for a year at the Levinsky Teachers' College, when it was still at the top of Ben-Yehuda Street in Tel Aviv. After the lessons we would sit in a nearby café and show each other drafts of poems. We spoke about our respective native kibbutzim in sad and angry words, like disappointed lovers. Since then Hayim got his doctorate in history and published a couple of thin volumes of poetry. Like many other poets, he has a small circle of friends and supporters—a critic or two, an editor at a publishing house, some childhood buddies—who help him sustain the illusion that it is still possible in Israel in the nineties, amid literature's fast-food stalls, for poetry to enjoy a real existence. Like many short men, he smiles a great deal, but the smiles don't soften his words. His fury about Israeli politics, from the fifties to the present, is low pitched and thought out, like metal which once glowed red hot and then cooled. What in me is a worldview, intuitions and empathy, he breaks down into dates and facts linked by sharp logic.

"I was going to send it to you to the United States," he says, taking out of his shoulder bag (a ranger's bag, characteristic of many ex-kibbutz men) his latest book of poetry. Two years ago he spent a couple of months in the south of France, and roved with his sensitive feelers over its colors, scents, and the taste of its women. I knew many of the poems from our past meetings. "You know I like your writing. The trouble is that in the relation between the Hayim I know and these poems, you are like a sculptor who starts to work on a huge rock, and eventually produces a delicate little statuette, a decorative object that leaves out all the stone. Don't you think that for a man like you, in this day and age, such poems are a bit self-indulgent?" Hayim gave me a wounded look. "Stop talking and give our guest something to drink," Dinah said, having made her way through to us. "The problem is," I said, unable to help myself, "is that you, your story, is much more interesting than your poems. I think that in fiction you'd have been able to leave more of yourself between the pages."

"Fiction?" he said, trying to sound casual, forgiving, making allowances for my bereavement, "Fiction I leave to you." In my last year at school I wrote a short story in which I tried to express the Schopenhauerian despair I was feeling. The plot revolved around a meeting between a young man who ran away from home and his sister, who tries to persuade him to return. I spent a whole evening going over it, and the only line I did not erase was something the sister says, telling her brother that life is worth living, despite everything: "The sword is also capable of mercy—it cannot cleave soft objects." I used that image in a poem that I published in *Davar* some months later. "Not a bad image," Hayim said. "But fiction can't be reduced to a single charged moment, and I have no idea how to construct a plot." "Nonsense. So write fiction which is a series of charged moments," Hayim snapped impatiently. He took his book from my hand and inscribed it in his large handwriting. "What must I do with you?" he said. "How many friends have I got to share my pleasure in a new book?"

A Walk

A Place

A.

Sunday. For the first time since my arrival I managed to sleep six consecutive hours. Taking advantage of my recovered freshness, I took my wife for a walk in Herzl Forest, where Hulda resided in its early years. In recent visits to my parents I made a point of spending an hour or two in the kibbutz archive. Our teachers and nurses used to tell us about those early days, when there was singing and dancing till dawn, but the old documents revealed a picture of conflicts, hardship, and poverty. Still, this knowledge did not prevent the rush of nostalgia I felt when we entered the forest. What was this feeling? A longing for childhood, for a world of solid, unequivocal meanings, and deep underneath, a yearning for all that has passed and is no more, a vague pining for a wondrous, mythical past, which is always, it seems, a wish to return to the womb. As if I didn't know: nostalgia is not merely longing for a happy past that will not return, but longing for the very stuff that beginnings are made of.

Though it was late March, the forest was not carpeted with greenery, as I remembered it—as if it has grown old and lost its capacity for renewal in the spring. My father came here sixty years ago, but of the sights that met his eyes, the only remnant was the Herzl House. Built at the end of the first decade of the century as a colonial country house, with a broad terrace and gothic windows, it came to serve as a home for a bunch of socialist pioneers, and when the kibbutz moved to its new site, it was left untenanted and desolate, a place of mildew, broken floor tiles, and bad odors. Only a huge bougainvillea colonized the staircase leading to the upper floor, its red blooms hanging above the black forest earth like a burst of fireworks. I was surprised to see that the house was being renovated for visitors, and for a moment felt annoyance, as if my childhood memories had given me a proprietary interest in it, or I'd found strangers in my bedroom.

The forest was my childhood's fairy-tale book. Old Hulda had left the Herzl House and the outline of its front courtyard, along with obscure longings for a right and natural world, where people breathed deep and sang and laughed wholeheartedly, slapping the tree trunks as though they were friends. "This was the silo pit," Elan said in a hushed voice, as if pointing to the king's palace. We failed to find any mushrooms, although it had rained that week, and after an hour's search we simply wandered about the forest. The large, smooth tiles he pointed at were warm as a body in the winter sunshine. For a moment it seemed as if a concentrated effort would enable one to penetrate the stone and reach the life that had been lived here not long ago.

The War of Independence had left paths outlined with whitewashed stones, twisted barbed-wire fences, and thousands of empty food cans—as if a magic palace had sunk out of sight, leaving only outlines and debris to remind us of our petty daily preoccupations and inspire permanent longing. On that distant Saturday we sat down to rest on one of the concrete platforms that were cast during the war to serve as floors for the soldiers' tents. Filaments of sunlight came through the pine canopy and hung camouflage webbing over the chilly surface. When I was four years old I stood with my kindergarten mates beside the cold storage and watched dusty soldiers riding in jeeps on the dirt road that crossed the kibbutz courtyard. I remember their wide smiles, as if the jeep drivers had been ordered to transfer a load of smiles from point A to point B. Elan leaned on the cold concrete, and I shut my eyes: sunburnt soldiers walked down the whitewashed paths, cleaned their rifles, or went to the faucets to wash the dust from their faces. Passing their comrades, their smiling eyes stood out of the dust like lips. "Let's go," said Elan, but I begged to stay a few minutes longer. His bored feet scraped the damp forest ground and exposed a layer of ash and scores of spent cartridges. Elan glanced at me (You-know-this-is-where-they-gathered-before-the-battle-that-broke-the-siege-of-Jerusalem, don't-you?) and looked down. We got up to leave.

The soldiers disappeared from the camp, and we were left with non-bullets buried beside the non-tents amid the non-paths. Years later, when Elan was in the army, we'd hike to the Galilee and visit the ruins of Sephori and the fort called Kawqab el-Hawa ("Star of the Winds"), which was still mostly below ground, but these did not give us a sense of something missed as did Herzl Forest. Here we had been so close to a full and true life, you could still smell the ashes, yet all that was left under the trees were the dirty concrete platforms and wandering, transparent, red-eyed soldiers. Here the opportunity was missed twice, and we knew there would never be another chance.

Today the carob tree beside Herzl House was hung with clusters of greenish carobs, like enormous pea pods, side by side with last year's fruits which had not been picked. I showed my wife the pepper-tree copse and the quarry on the hillside (the forest had grown over it; the magic cave on its margin, with its quarried bluestone roof, was plugged up), and the pine tree curved like a camel's hump. When I was small I rode on that camel tree all over the forest. We walked on to the avenue of sycamores that led to Herzl House, and I soon spotted the site of the old silo pit. But the magic chest of my childhood lay empty. The mature eye saw only a small wood, with bare outcrops and thorn bushes among its trees. When I was a little boy the avenue of palm trees opposite Herzl House reached up to the sky. Now the sky was very remote.

B.

You can reach the forest from the narrow asphalt road that grazes its southern edge, or from behind, through the palm tree avenue that crosses the fields and reaches the forest from the north. These two approaches made for two quite different walks. The first was the formal, public one which set out on holidays or Saturdays from the kibbutz gate. It was implicitly understood that coming out of the gate you turned left, towards the forest, and not right, in the direction of the Youth Corps farm and the village of Ekron. The other walk, like a lining of a dress, started from the rear gate of the kibbutz. A rusty misshapen gate led to a dirt road that turned east and passed between the olive grove and the vineyards, and ended in the palm tree avenue that led to the forest. Only three hundred yards separated this gate from that of the kibbutz, but this little distance divided two such very dissimilar experiences, that most members chose one of these walks and never attempted the other. Elan and I used to follow the road on our way to the forest to look for mushrooms. On my own, I used to go out through the kibbutz back gate in the afternoon or after dark, a skinny boy inflated with loneliness, convinced that the entire world could see his loneliness, and that this was the stuff great men were made of.

Few vehicles ever passed on the narrow asphalt road that led to the forest, and Hulda members walked on it as if it were a broad pavement, with the comfortable assurance of a landowner strolling about his estate. Even Ozer Huldai and his wife, who took the kibbutz paths at a brisk trot, always rushing to some meeting, here sauntered slowly, leaning back, raising their knees, relishing their leisure, or perhaps demonstrating to the rest of the community how to enjoy a free hour, especially on a day of rest, and moreover on a road that had once been a muddy track. They would greet Elan and me ceremoniously, according to the occasion, enunciating every word clearly and concluding with a solemn nod, as though to say, other people use these greetings casually, whereas we mean every word. The asphalt road, the signpost indicating the presence of the community and the cultivated fields, everything created an illusion of a settled, secure world, and the members would walk down the road in couples, like lovers presenting themselves in the high street, relishing the holiday and the wide-open spaces. Their white sabbath shirts brightened their eyes and softened their features.

The signpost saying "Hulda" stood rigidly firm, but to them it was a flapping banner, and their memories of the early years in this place further elevated the festive pleasure. In the 1940s Arabs from the nearby villages sometimes mined the dirt road, or fired on the kibbutz vehicle driving slowly on its rough surface. Halfway to the forest was the stony hill, at the foot of which were buried the commune's first casualties, and the solemn black letters on the square tomb, marking the grave of "Our comrades, victims of battle and fieldmine," evoked sadness and suppressed gladness, intensifying the festive feeling.

Between the stony hill and the forest the evergreen mass of the olive grove stretched along the left side of the road. It had been planted at the beginning of the century, and by now each tree had a distinctive face which gazed at the strollers with its black trunk eyes. Though the grove bore fruit every two or three years, in a cycle no one understood, the members felt a great affection for it, because it had been there when they arrived, and was their first source of income. The kibbutz paper carried paeans of praise for the olive's vitality, which no drought, uprooting, or fire could defeat. The olive harvest and the sorting of the preserved fruit were labor intensive, and it was often necessary to declare a general call-up to finish the job in time. But as they strolled past, the members did not see the tree with their hands, which had picked the olives, but with their inner eyes, as though the olives were perceived in two different locations in the brain on weekdays and holidays, and were now an abstract symbol, synonymous with loyalty and devotion.

The kibbutz members would stop on the edge of the forest, hesitate, then turn around and walk back. Memory was kind to them. The eight years they spent in the forest were a time of utter poverty, lack of work, and brackish water that was insufficient for drinking and bathing. In 1936, Max Nurock, the secretary of the British High Commissioner, went hunting in the hills around Hulda and was shocked by a huddle of huts, tents, and animal sheds around a dirty, miry yard. His friend Dr Burger, riding beside him, glanced at the settlers and said, patronizingly, that he thought the place was used for breeding horses. Nurock, the highest-placed Jew in the British administration of Palestine, stated in a letter to the settlement department of the Jewish Agency that he had never seen such dirt and neglect in the most backward Arab village. Portions of this letter were quoted in an official report of a representative of the Histadrut Sick Fund, who was sent there soon afterwards, following an epidemic of typhoid fever which brought down most of the members and killed three of them. But after the move to the new Hulda, weeds appeared and covered the wretchedness, and the communal memory retained only the scent of dew on the pine needles, the pine scent in the sweat of the dancers when festivals were celebrated in the square in front of Herzl House, and the pale mauve cups of the first crocuses after the rain (these hastened to appear ahead of their leaves, long before the anemones, whose crimson leaves were so perfectly symmetrical that they caused a twinge of strange sadness).

During the War of Independence Herzl House was the command post of the Israeli forces in the area, and the hundreds of soldiers who camped here, and the hundreds of supply trucks which set out from here to Jerusalem, painted the forest with a new coat of memories and pride, and the days of forced idleness and poverty were buried under the piles of empty cans and the paths outlined with whitewashed pebbles. The forest continued to grow at its own pace, reflecting the quantities of rain that fell on it, the degrees of dryness and heat and the depth of the topsoil, and the treetops rustled quietly, self-sufficiently. The passage of time also conferred the forest's dimensions on the life that had been lived amidst its trees, concealing the yawning gulf between the dreams and aspirations and the life that had actually been lived on its rocky ground. Kibbutz memory recalled the nineteen-thirties as the golden age of the kibbutz, and the members spoke of them with a wistful smile, as though recollecting a distant love. Reaching the forest, they would stop, hesitating whether to walk toward Herzl House, reluctant to step on their finest memories.

Elan and I, however, had no qualms about entering the forest. We hurried first to the cluster of pepper trees south of the House, and the sycamore avenue which went down the slope on the north side toward the Arab well at the edge of the forest, searching all the while for mushrooms. The only ones we trusted were the pine boletus, whose caps had the golden tint of the fur of wild hares. They soon became very scarce, and we frequently returned empty-handed. Often the ones we found were wormy or waterlogged and rotting, but the fresh ones, three or four days old, would reward us for the long search with the perfect, intense yellow (the essence of yellowness, discovered only by the weary and persistent eye) that was hidden under their skin.

On the other side of the kibbutz, where the dirt road led to the palm tree avenue, there were no festive feelings or old memories to get between the walker and the view of the plantations and fields, and in the clear air it was easy to see if the olive trees were bearing this year and if the grapes were ripe for harvesting. The serious expressions on the faces of the strollers showed that leisure time could also be used to check up on the fields and groves. They would later complain in the kibbutz paper about agricultural implements left to rust in the field. Also through this gate came young couples who wished to be unobserved, and likewise couples whose room had become too close to contain their words or their silence also used this escape hatch. It was possible to walk side by side without speaking, and the gentle rise of the hills, creating an illusion of deep breathing (as though the ground was practicing for the mountains of Jerusalem, eas-ily seen from this place), blended into their silence and tempered it.

In winter and spring the ground in the kibbutz was carpeted with the intense green of the winter weeds, and in the edges of the fields and the rims of the fruit-trees the wild chrysanthemums flowered above the yolk-yellow marigolds, as if demonstrating shades of yellow. The feathery heads of the chicory and the blue centaury thronged around them, and the pink flax—its delicate tint creating a false impression of fragility—writhed amid the silver-green flower heads of the thorns and thistles. The walkers who had come from the main gate would stop beside the road and on the stony hill, trying to befriend flowers they had not known in their native lands, like strangers trying to make friends with the locals, and returned home with a small bunch of wildflowers.

On the other side of the kibbutz the walkers walked briskly along the dirt road, every now and then entering the vineyard and firmly uprooting a handful of weeds which had escaped the plow. This was no place for mooning over the past, or admiring the exquisite blue eyes of the tiny flowers that sheltered in the shade of the olive trees. From this side it was possible to see the Latrun ridge, which reminded the walkers that the Jor-danian border was a few kilometers away. The Arab village Saidun was plowed over soon after the War of Independence, and vines grew over its former houses and fields, but some ruins remaining on the hills infused a menace too subtle to be tackled. (Two days before, when Hayim inter-rupted his translation of my parents' letters to make us both tea, he replied to my question about the Arab village: "Why didn't we try to find out what happened to the villagers we used to know before the war?—Because their leaders called on them to leave till the war was over, and that was that." I couldn't believe my ears. Gordonia preached the constant renewal of the inner life, but the disciples' loyalty to its leaders was gradually replaced by a lazy, pigheaded loyalty to all the government's slogans.) A few days before the Suez War, a number of "fidayun" crossed the border and blew up a kibbutz building, leaving behind terror and scuffed traces. The Six-Day War pushed back the Jordanian border, and Hulda found itself, unprepared, in the center of the country.

C.

We walked back to the kibbutz on the dirt road that led to the palm-tree avenue. A year after the Suez War the Pioneer Corps held a grand spectacle in the field beside the avenue. The master of ceremonies, speaking from the high podium, intoned the achievements of the Pioneer Corps in solemn tones like a radio announcer. The audience, who had assembled from all the nearby settlements, sat on the ground, waiting for the parade and the parachute jumping. On the ground before us, near the roped-off enclosure, sat a number of Yemenite women, like the ones who worked in the kibbutz in the summer harvests. We glanced at each other and without a word went past and sat down in front of them. "Now you're blocking our view," said one of them, whether in complaint or to inform us of the difficulty. Her soft utterance, in the voice of a woman who knows she is on alien ground, only widened the grins: Did you see that?

The olive grove which had adjoined the palm-tree avenue was uprooted long ago, and now long rows of watermelons stretched in its place. The dirt road had been diverted to bypass the vineyards, which spread eastward. Right in the middle of the fields, to the northwest, a solitary buckthorn tree remained which many years ago served Elan and me as the signpost of the narcissus field. (The wide gully that meandered among the hills was lined with pebbles that scattered the white twinkle of the narcissi over the field, up to the cirrus clouds floating over the hills and the wintry, narcissus-like moon above them. What did we do with the dozens of flowers we picked? I can't remember. As though that walk and that Saturday began at the north gate and ended there, several narcissus hours later, only to arouse in me now an unexpected nostalgia for the boy-I-was.)

The track went down the incline toward the kibbutz, and all at once revealed the red roofs of the veteran members' houses, the cowsheds, and the cemetery cypresses. A small habitation, entirely within its boundaries. It begins here, with the veteran housing, and ends over there, behind the sheep pen. It is plainly visible in the clear winter air: in the beginning was the word. In the dining hall and the members' rooms and tents, the words Zionism, Equality, and Manual Labor were as tangible as a loaf of bread, a hoe, and a pickax. Sixty years later all that remains are a loaf of bread, a table, the cracking walls of the veterans' houses, and some weeding and hoeing in the fields.

Down on the main pavement leading to the dining hall I met Sarah, Yossi's mother, leaning on a zimmer frame, on which hung two big bags of groceries from the shop beside the dining hall. Her face twitched, like a patient in a hospital corridor embarrassed by his nudity. "What we've come to," she said, as if that was the one text she had prepared for our chance encounters.

After lunch Mom asked me to drive her to Father's grave. She stood there for a few moments, her head lowered, while I walked among the rows of tombstones. The bitter scent of the cypresses was a childhood odor, and the Hebrew phrases on the stones—"One of Hulda's founders and builders"—was the language of my childhood. Most of the kibbutz founders have already left this world. Only in such a small community can you clearly observe the patient, precise strokes of death's scythe: a whole generation marched from the veterans' houses to the headstone neighborhood. Here lay side by side the asphalt road walkers and the dirt-road ones, whose paths had never mingled in life. The offenders and the offended, the loud and the reticent, finally achieved the equality and cooperation that had evaded them when they lived. Mom stood silent, then suddenly said in a conversational tone, as if to arouse him from his old man's doze, "Avremalé is here too, you know." She took my arm and murmured, "I wish I could be sure that he knows you came." Between my father's grave and the next there was a space left. Mom took three steps and stood in front of the portion of black earth waiting for her. A slight, girlish smile flitted on her face. It had never occurred to me before, but now I found, to my own surprise, that I too would like to end my journey in that place.

A Nocturnal Chat

Mom: Does he talk to you about his stories?

My brother: Stories? He said something about writing a novel.

My sister: Stories, he's always talking about the stories he'd like to write about our childhood.

My brother: About us? What is there to write about us?

Mom: Some kind of memoir, I think. Pity Father won't get to see it. He tried so much to show Avremalé that he also knew about literature, that he'd read Frishman and Sholem Asch and Scholem Aleichem.

Circles

Children's Stories

A.

Mom is full of remorse. "I don't deserve it," she repeats whenever Elan, Dinah, and I want to do something for her. She is all too willing to admit her sins of omission and of commission. But she defends Father with all her might: "He was an orphan and you never understood him." When I was in kindergarten there was an epidemic of mumps, and to avoid it spreading to the adults, the children were confined to the children's houses and forbidden to be with their parents. The parents would come in the evening and chat with the kids through the windows. One evening Mom couldn't come and Father came instead. I was feeling hungry for some reason, and asked if he could bring me a sandwich (perhaps I was not really hungry, but only addressed the wrong person: being a skinny child, it was my way of communicating with Mom, and I must have thought the request would please him). He would have had to go to the dining hall to get the sandwich, and to my surprise he sounded displeased. He said his head hurt, and I quickly gave up. I recall his resentful expression when he spoke of his headache, and discover that Mom is right: it is the face of a hurt child, who feels that too much is expected of him. Would this memory have been different if I'd known about his being an orphan? Who can tell. Childhood hurts do not grow up.

Since he could not expect love from us, he tried in his old age to win one of its handmaidens—compliments. At the age of seventy he began to learn to paint, and spent his free time in front of a canvas. He was a fairly good craftsman and able to copy the work of others, and even to paint his favorite landscapes. He had a good eye: the portrait of Mom he painted when she was seventy did not look like her, but ten years later it became evident that he saw her better than we did—she increasingly resembled her image on the wall. Whenever I came to the kibbutz he would show me his latest paintings, trying by various means to extract a word of praise or encouragement. I hardened my heart, as if I'd be violating some abstract aesthetic principle by giving him a little praise. Elan and Dinah, too, were unable to hide their disdain when he fished for compliments (my wife alone, the only one of us who actually studied painting, had no difficulty finding the right words to satisfy his hunger). Mom was right, he was an orphaned man.

B.

The boy played in the snow with his new friends. Evening fell, but no one came to look for him. Finally the cold and the dark overcame him and he dashed over a number of wooden fences and went into his house. His asthmatic mother, his grandmother, and five brothers and sisters were sitting around the table. Not long before, after his father's sudden death, the family had moved into this place, and now the worried-looking grandmother and mother were listening to the financial plans proposed by the older brothers, fifteen and sixteen years old respectively. He knew these preoccupied expressions and realized that the family circle would not open to greet him. Going quietly to the stove to warm his feet, he walked past his aunt Nehama, who had come to help with advice. To his surprise, she embraced him and tried to warm his frozen cheeks between her palms. In another few years he would fall in love with a well-off girl who would love him too. He would not say much about his childhood, but he did tell his wife time and again about that warm hug, and quoted the exact words of affection his aunt murmured in his ear.

The boy stayed with friends of his parents in Netanya. When he was in first grade he came with his mother and made friends with the beach and with the hosts' daughter, who was his age. In subsequent years he came every summer for a week or ten days. He enjoyed the beach and the big house and the family's quiet children (it was easy to fall asleep to the soft sounds of the household on the other side of the glass door). He enjoyed the taste of the grapes and the watermelon flavor of the setting sun. The sun would stop still at half past seven, and he would watch it, amazed. It seemed as if the quicksilver light on the warm sea would never sink. One day a woman joined them for lunch. Before leaving she looked at the boy and said in Yiddish, "What a beautiful boy." He understood the words, but not this use of them. His teachers and nurses had taught him that words must be used directly and precisely, and he was accustomed to direct and precise words. He remembered the first time he recognized himself in the low mirror in the bathroom of the children's house: the blue eyes were all right, and the thinness didn't bother him (it was sinewy thinness, and he could already outrun the other kids), but the freckles on his face were something he detested in other children's faces. He clearly recalled the shrinking feeling, the reluctance to believe, and the transition from I-can't-stand-it to if-it's-me-it-can't-be-so-bad. He was a skinny kid and had no illusions about being beautiful, and in his heart he thanked that woman and always remembered her warm smile.

On the sixth day of the shivah his mother told him about the hug that Aunt Nehama had given his father, rest his soul. His wife stared at him in amazement.

A Family Picture

After lunch my wife and I look through the skimpy family album. The faces that look out at us in black and white reflect an existence so remote that my mind struggles to believe that once upon a time I was that child.

When I was a child, a photograph, particularly a family photograph, was a rare and special event. In the children's houses the nurses kept festive outfits for the children to wear when they went with their parents to the nearest town, Rehovot, for a studio picture. "What pudgy cheeks you had," Raheli laughs, pointing at one of the few family pictures in the album.

1947. Elan is seven; I am about two and a half. We're both neatly combed and our shirts are buttoned all the way up. Father, on the other hand, knows that he need not break his habit and button his shirt all the way up, even on this special occasion. The jacket he had brought from Bendery ten years ago, kept for such events, is as good as new. My cheeks still have a babyish roundness about them, like downy chicks. Mom's hairstyle has changed drastically since she came to the kibbutz, and the irregular parting in her hair shows that she took more pains with her children's hair than with her own. Father has the same shock of hair he always had.

My parents look straight ahead, smiling faintly. Elan and I are interested in something we've just spotted in a corner of the room. Nevertheless, the picture creates a momentary sense of family framework. My ingratiating posture suggests that I'm conscious of the attention, the solemnity of the occasion, and the significance of the special clothes. In this photograph, which was my favorite in childhood, Mom's dark clothes and mine join us into a single mass, and you can't tell where her body ends and mine begins. The angle of the photograph creates the impression that my father, who is carrying me, is giving me his hand, and as if my head is leaning with infantile confidence on his shoulder.

Like those bride-and-bridegroom photographs taken on the eve of the wedding, posed against the sea and the setting sun, here we are, mother and father and two sons, well dressed and close together, a single, defined photographic entity, "Family."

A Will

"Avremalé, I want you to promise me something, that you will all keep in touch. That is . . . ," she gropes for the right word, gives up, chooses another term. "That is my wish." She looked at me closely to be sure I understood what she was getting at. "In my family everyone kept in touch, and that gave me strength for the rest of my life. My father's brother Hayim had a soap factory, and because of the chemicals he was using he built himself a house outside town. Hayim, you know, was the grandfather of Ami, from Kibbutz Ayalon? (How come I never knew this? Did they tell me and I forgot, because my parents' family never interested me much? I try to work out the relationship between me and Ami and fail. The only relatives I have known since childhood have been uncles and people from my parents' hometowns. Ami, at any rate, is real family.) You should have seen what a vineyard he had beside his house. In the summer he would send Vassilka, their Christian maid, several times a week with a basket of grapes for us. Such big black grapes, with the dew still on them. On weekends and holidays he and his wife and all their children would come over, and there was so much warmth, kissing and hugging, and how are you and how you've grown. Mother would serve tea and cakes she'd baked and jam that she made. We used to play and laugh together, and our parents looked on. Not far from us lived father's parents, Mordechai and Malka, and they visited us and we them. I was still a child when Grandpa Mordechai died, and my father's brother, Baruch, carried me to their house. Did my father have other brothers and sisters? Sure he did—there were Yosef and Hinda and Hannah-Gittel, but I never met them. They emigrated to Brazil in 1918. (So I have family in Brazil? What's going on here? My father's death is enlarging my family. Suddenly there's a family that needs only to be located.) We had a big house, and after the shivah they prepared a room for Malka, with its own bathroom and everything. But she had her meals with us, downstairs. She had a bedside cupboard, like they have in hospitals, and she always kept sweet things in it. One night my mother saw that her light was on, so she knocked on her door and went in, and found grandma sitting on the bed, eating a cake. She asked what was the matter, and grandma said, *Ich mach eich a gezunte mameh*—which means, more or less, I'm making you a healthy mama. For years afterwards mother used to tell this story, and everyone laughed. We had a big family. You knew you were not alone. Here, for some reason, the family connection was not encouraged. When I came it wasn't even proper for married couples to hold hands when walking through the kibbutz or entering the dining hall. God forbid that a husband and wife should take a bit of the kibbutz warmth for themselves. God forbid that a children's nurse should show a bit more warmth to her own child than to the other children. Avremalé, write down Elan's and Dinah's birth dates. There's only three of you. That is my wish."

Completions

Two Possible Stories

A. EXCELLENCE AT EIGHTY-FIVE

The disintegration of the kibbutz as well as his own body made my father in his final years more bitter and cantankerous than ever. "Do you find any comfort in the knowledge," I asked him in August 1995, on my last visit that summer vacation, "that you were a pioneer, that you've been a kibbutz member all these years?" He remained silent for a long time, and I shrank in my seat, wondering if he had heard my actual question. Then he looked up and asked in a wondering tone, "Do you really want an answer?" I nodded uneasily, and he said, "I'm glad that I passed the test, that I held out." The phone rang—Hava, Mom's friend from her home town, was asking after Father's health (Mom clutched the receiver the way a person who learned to drive late in life clutches the steering wheel). "Do you remember her husband?" she asked me after she hung up. Her eyes glistened, as they always did when speaking of the dead. "He died in time," said Father angrily. His voice sounded rough and dull, like a cracked earthen pot.

The day after he arrived Father was sent to work in the orange grove, to clear out the "saucers" at the base of the young trees and dig "saucers" for new trees. Though the hoe blistered his hand, he continued to work till dark and as he walked back to the kibbutz on the muddy track he imagined that the members were commenting on his diligence, and felt a wave of affection for them and for himself. Thereafter he devoted his life in this place to building the kibbutz and his own reputation, and saw no

176

conflict between the two aims. His way of achieving excellence was hard and slow: wrapping thick paper around the trunks of the apple trees, to protect them from the gnawing hares, painstakingly cultivating the trees, pruning their foliage, tree by tree, row after row, thinning the budding fruit, branch after branch, harvesting the ripe fruit, and sorting it in the late summer and fall. And so day after day, decade after decade, for forty years. "I am so happy that my great efforts have won me the reputation of a good strong worker," he wrote to my mother with undisguised pride six months after his arrival.

But now there was no pride in his voice when he said he was glad he had withstood the test of those long years. Everything was going against him—the young kibbutz members who calculated profit and loss behind his back, as though they themselves were impervious to aging, the doctors who couldn't ease his pains, and the government that preferred to invest its limited resources in the health of the young. All his life he had looked for ways to prove himself, to achieve excellence. How could he do so now, when his legs had turned to water? When he was twenty he crisscrossed Russia, visiting the cells of the Gordonia movement, and later would extend his journeys by hundreds of miles in order to see his beloved in Bricheva. For decades he walked twice a day to the apple orchard and back, worked all day on his feet, pruning, thinning, or picking, and now his legs turned against him and confined him to his bed and the dining table opposite the television. How can a kibbutz member achieve excellence when the wrappings around his body are malodorous?

When I visited him at the Hartzfeld Hospital during the Christmas vacation of 1996, he was no longer a kibbutz member but an old man with the fear of death in his eyes. After so many years in which his kibbutz membership was the core of his identity, he was surprised to discover how little he thought about the kibbutz in the vague hospital time, demarcated only by the meals and the doctors' rounds. His mind, which remained clear, was now preoccupied with planning how to move his huge red hands very carefully so as to relieve the pain caused by the drip tubes that went into his shoulders, with evaluating the effect of the tablets on his pain and considering what he would say to the doctor when he stopped on his daily round.

"Well, how is your hero doing?" the ward sister asked Mom when she passed the nurses' station. "Amazing how he never leaves a crumb on the plate." Her voice reached his room in a subdued, conspiratorial tone, and it suddenly came to him that the great division lay not between those who carried out the mission and those who fell by the wayside, between industrious and lazy workers, but between the living and the dead, and he wondered how he could have failed to see this obvious truth for so many years. And with the same sudden clarity of vision, as though a cataract had fallen from his ailing eyes, he saw how he could still achieve excellence, and was not concerned that there was now a complete discrepancy between his interest and that of the kibbutz, for whose welfare he had labored for half a century. I sat beside his bed (this was my last visit: I went directly from the hospital to the airport), and he wished to say something to me. He was excited or impatient. The tremor in his body reached his mouth, the words wallowed in his mouth, and I had to complete the broken syllables that came out. Talking exhausted him, and he laid his head back on the pillow and closed his eyes. When I said I had to leave he mustered all his strength and said slowly, straining to pronounce every word: "We'll meet in the summer, as always." He squeezed my hand, and I stooped and for the first time embraced his cold shoulders.

B. A VISIT IN MARCH

"What about Avremalé?" his wife asked in a low voice, and Dinah replied, "I left him a message but I think he's already on his way." Avremalé? he wondered, how come Avremalé, now, in winter? The pain in his legs had eased and now the legs seemed very long and far away, but the pressure in his chest grew worse and he breathed with difficulty. Then, as sleep overcame him, he was glad that he'd survived another semester and would soon see his son arrive for the summer vacation.

These past weeks a car would come from the kibbutz to take his wife home after she had given him his supper. He spent the long evening hours in the dim hospital light with his children. When they were young he would return from the apple orchard at dusk, shower and rest a little, then go to the dining hall for supper. After the meal he would hang on in the dining hall near the table of the person responsible for the work roster, amid arguments and cigarette smoke. He was never allocated as many workers as he needed, and he always had to explain and plead, but he enjoyed these discussions. Other members, sitting at other tables, were exchanging opinions and sections of the morning paper, chatting and laughing like schoolchildren at recess. Now he rejoiced in his children and did not know what he would have done without them in the lonely evenings, amid the patients' cries and the nurses' scolding. With his eyes shut he would take Dinah by the hand and walk with her to the sheep pen and explain the connection between the surrounding spring and the newborn lambs, and carry her on his shoulders and tickle her neck with an unpracticed hand. When they got back he kissed her rosy cheek, and she wiped the kiss off and complained that his face was prickly, and her giggles relieved the pressure in his chest. While snores arose from the other beds in the room, and in the hallway the ward sister was giving last instructions to the night-shift nurses, he told his children about the refugees who swam across the Dnieper at the end of the First World War, then told them about his father's sudden death, when he was only nine years old, and wondered if he should tell them about the great fear that seized him then, the anxious nausea he felt for weeks on end when he comprehended the extent of the disaster and could not imagine how his older brothers would be able to support his mother and grandmother and his younger brothers, while Elan gazed at him with the quiet wisdom of his blue eyes, and Dinah and Avram snuggled up to him as children snuggle up to their father.

Now and then he was unable to visualize the faces of his children and their images dissolved in his mind like cloud shapes. Then the borderline between sleep and waking became blurred, as well as between pain and nonpain, and his wife's face floated before his eyes and disappeared, and all that remained was the continuous effort to pull masses of air into his lungs. He opened his eyes momentarily and saw the male nurse who always came to shave the patients for the Sabbath, and knew that it was Friday, and for a moment it seemed to him that he could hear not only his wife's voice in the hallway, but also Dinah's and Elan's. "What about Avremalé?" his wife was asking behind the door, and Dinah replied, "I left him a message but I think he's already on his way." The voices reached him across a vast distance, and the joy about his son's forthcoming visit passed through him like the light of a car flashing across a dark room. It was replaced by a spasm of complaint and terror (that-sensitive-kid-who-always-had-to-be-treated-special; he-couldn't-make-the-time-and-will-come-straight-to-the-cemetery). It seemed to him that both the joy and the grumbling were taking place outside his body, and only a thin thread of air connected them to him, and then it snapped.

Crowding

A.

Sunday night. It's raining outside and indoors there is a damp, Israeli chill. As a child I loved to hear the raindrops pattering on the roof like pigeons' feet (they always arrived late, after a long wait). The electric heater hardly warms the bedroom. Raheli's eyes are closing, but I am far from sleepy. I can't get rid of Lavon's statement about the Gordonians, those children of the poor and ignorant, which I had come across earlier in the evening. Only the total break between us and our parents can explain how we could have been taken in by the slogans of equality and cooperation, how we failed to see that they hid a sharp division between the powerful and the humble. Most of the members did not participate in the ideological discussions in the local paper, and hardly ever opened their mouths in the general meetings. Industrious and obedient, they went to work every morning, a permanent expression of dark puzzlement on their faces. I see them standing at the faucets beside the dining hall door, rinsing their hands again and again, peering at each other in silence, with a solemn, choirboy expression that demonstrated their devotion to the kibbutz ideal.

My father, who had had only primary schooling but taught himself a good deal, and who at an early age ran the Gordonia branch in his town, found himself in the most vulnerable position: belonging to neither class, suspicious and critical of both. Elan was four months short of six years when his class was about to start the first grade of school. Ozer Huldai decided that Elan should wait for two years, until the next group started first grade. It meant separating him from the group he had grown up with, and that he would be nearly eight when he started first grade. Father tried to argue and explain that this would not be a good thing. "Where did you learn that?" Ozer snapped at him at the general meeting, deliberately aiming his whip at my father's soft underbelly. Thereafter Father never dared oppose him in public, but secretly stored his hurts and hates. How clear everything is now: that retreat from the battlefield and the withdrawal into a corner to lick real or imaginary wounds was what turned the fine mechanism that produced my youthful poems. Elan and Dinah, too, in their respective ways, were also caught up in that mechanism.

Now, at long last, I understand why my father, who never took any interest in my schooling so long as I was in the kibbutz, was so happy about my academic degrees. Did my academic gown helped to cover his childhood's tailor's clothes? I fear not. I found out on my walk to my first children's house that only the person who kicked you can take away that kick. The chilling lines from the poem about the foundling come to my mind: "I'll go back to my mother's house / as the ball rolls back to the kicking foot." These words freeze my marrow even more than the cold air.

My wife's sleeping breaths, normally so catching, do not help me this time. I open the Gordonia book and read by the dim light from the front room. Lavon, states Comrade Israel Bitman soporifically, did not at first believe that it was essential to bring the movement he had created into the general kibbutz movement. Later he decided in favor of establishing small, selective communes rather than large-sized kibbutzim. (Did he think that only in a small commune of no more than fifty members would it be possible to cultivate his ignorant young people?) The official reasoning was that only in a small, intimate framework would the individual be able to realize the fullness of life, as preached by A. D. Gordon. I am seized with rage: by what alchemical principles did Lavon imagine that the poor lads he had recruited would here recover from their childhood hurts and the insults of their youth? Here, of all places? Shut in with each other's grievances in a small isolated community, surrounded by Arab villages? Such a way of life is meant for angels, for saints who have expunged all traces of power hunger and material greed. Did Lavon really and truly believe that contact with the soil of Eretz Israel would transmute these dross metals into gold? Last summer my wife and I, on a visit to the Huleh nature reserve, passed by Kibbutz Massadah, another Gordonia commune. We went in and for a couple of hours wandered about, horrified by the sight of the crushed, desolate community. The giant ficus trees, their branches amputated back to the trunk, emphasized the wretchedness of the cracking houses and the neglected courtyard. It was heartrending: another ghost courtyard, another dream structure neglected and crumbling. The entire kibbutz movement is in crisis, but the Gordonia communes have been the first to collapse.

B.

Picture a group of people in a house, not a very large house—each couple has a corner, or at best a room to itself. Bathroom and toilets are communal, and in the public showers a wall separates the women's section from the men's. And this is a way of life, not a temporary shelter. They know that tomorrow they will again rub against each other, touching, overhearing, catching an incautious look, having conflicting wishes and needs, and knowing that next month the communal clothing store will again issue them the same work clothes and the same white Sabbath shirts. Very soon they realize that next year they will still overhear their next-door neighbor abusing his wife and will see her walking past, clearing her throat to suppress a moan. They make no attempt to ease the crowding. In the early years they do not even own personal clothes—every Friday the members are issued identical bundles of clothes, until at last they are forced to admit that the girth of their waist or length of their arms simply do not obey the splendid rules they have laid down for themselves. The dining hall contains massive wooden tables with six chairs each. The dining hall workers make sure that no one goes to a free table until the others are filled up. Most of the members obey the rule, but some soon learn to maneuver things so as to end up at a friendly table: they take longer to wash their hands at the entrance, linger before the notice board, take another look at the day's mail.

Do you see the picture? Now watch what happens. This uniformed crowding threatens their individuality and they begin to defend themselves against it, to put up barriers, and the more they feel threatened, the thicker the barriers, as in a simple law of physics. At the same time, they each try to establish their individuality—in hard work, in social activity, in self-isolation. Nobody warns them that the more they try to establish a distinct personality, the more they lose it, merely replacing a face with a mask. And all the time, while walking to work, while at work and on their way home, they are watched by the big eye of this house. They adopt a blank expression, rather like people entering a room full of strangers. They grow like plants that have been sown too close together—with bent and twisted branches, with strange excretions, fantastic extensions. Their children will grow up together in the children's houses like grains that fell from a torn bag and sprouted one on top of the other, entangled and distorted together, incapable of standing by themselves.

So they grow together and unconsciously they stop conversing with each other and instead report each other's doings. "Blumah's nipples are hopelessly cracked," says Shifra to Genia in the kitchen. "Breast feeding has become a nightmare for her." "Henya is pregnant, at last," says Genia. "Miriam has just heard from her younger brother in Russia, after years when she didn't hear at all," throws in Sarka. When she steps out to fetch groceries from their storage shed behind the dining hall, the others will exchange remarks and speculations about her son, who has a stammer.

From month to month, from year to year, the eyes harden, glaze over, become opaque. The instinct of survival whispers to them that in such crowding it is best not to heed every moan, especially since it is heard but faintly across the barrier—perhaps it is only the wind, or a creaking tree branch. Especially since after the Second World War they slowly find out that the families they had left behind were killed by poison or fire or hunger, and now and then frightful sobs break out in one of the rooms and cannot be soothed all night long. The following days or weeks the one who cried looks pallid and must be treated like an invalid.

They conduct their lives rationally—this one teaches and that one drives, this one works in the field and that one is a children's nurse. But the crowding means that their paths keep crossing, and here every person is both proprietor and tenant, and this novel and confusing arrangement gives rise to illusions and grievances. They are easily offended and do not readily forgive, because a grievance lends strength, something to use in future accounting. On every back is pinned a sheet of his or her sins from the moment they arrived, and they are incapable of forgetting, incapable of forgiving, because crowding repels forgiveness as water repels flames.

They have come to this house with an explicit program—here they would raise a new human being with a new heart: what's mine is yours, what's yours is mine. How easy, how delightful to grow accustomed to the idea that what is yours is mine (a sweet momentary feeling, as though an ancient prohibition or menace has been removed). No one admits that it is harder to accustom oneself to the notion that what's mine is yours than to what's yours is mine, because they believe in words, being ideological sort of people, and use them as a mirror to measure themselves against. In the name of these principles they don't cease to rasp and abrade each other with advice and criticism. Their parents, who had lived under alien roofs and alien skies, gave Yiddish exquisitely fine feelers for sensing and evading every obstacle in their path. Yiddish was the oil that smoothed the movement of a fine mechanism—a secret, allusive language, a language for having the cake and eating it, full of winks and hints. Here, on their own land, the members relish the air of freedom and the liberty to use direct speech, and they wield Hebrew like a hammer, fling it like gravel, to tell the person sitting opposite them in the dining hall exactly what they think of him or her, with never a compliment, because crowding and compliments are as mutually exclusive as oil and water.

Here they will raise a new man, cultivate a new nose. The workers come from the cowshed and sheep pen straight to the dining hall with the smell of dung hanging about them like a cloud of flies. Gordon's praise for simplicity and modesty are interpreted as an instruction to avoid all toiletries. If a women attempts to use scent to disguise the summer smell of sweat, it is at once noticed by the house's keen sense of smell. Crowding is an excellent conductor of rumor, and gossip ensures that the fragrant experiment is not repeated. Most of the women adopt a short and simple hairstyle, and with their dry sunburnt faces they soon resemble the menfolk.

In addition, they read the movement's daily paper and its pamphlets. The words Zionism, Equality, and Socialism are as tangible in the rooms as fire and knives. They believe in the ability of words to resolve disputes and mend hearts, and are forever denouncing, verbally or in writing, every perceived deviation or wrong. To read their articles in the local paper, you might think that the wheels of this world are turned by the continuous tension between justice and injustice, between what must be done and what has not been done. They transmit this language to their children, like a genetic defect.

Can you see the picture? And don't forget the huge step they took when they came here. "We have come to this land / to build and be rebuilt here," they chant, as if it were a prayer, hoping to grow a new heart in this place, a heart free from desire for power, from material greed. The prayer produces a momentary miracle: their voices are borne on the air with the sparks from the campfire, and the sweat welds arm to arm, shoulder to shoulder. The sweat strips away the old cells, and they try to extend the moment, to stretch it like a skin. And the more their old hearts, the hearts of their parents, still pound in their veins, the more loudly they denounce their comrades who cling to old habits.

The festivals are the only times when they beam at each other, as if the festival brings its own generous space with enough room for everyone. They greet each other with broad gestures and stand around chatting, as if they have not seen each other for a long time. When they go to town to visit relatives or for a short holiday, their eyes look innocent, wondering and friendly, somehow thawed, like the face of a beautiful woman coming in from the street into a friend's house.

C.

I'm cold. I'm shivering with cold and sadness. It was easier to bear the anger at the kibbutz than the sorrow for its collapse. My eyes are sore from tiredness (which doesn't lead to sleep but reverberates between the temples which are joined by the beam of a headache) and the dim light. "I have been struck by the worst blow," my father said to us on one of our last visits in 1995, pointing to his useless legs. We were sitting around the table, and he sank into a self-pitying silence. "What do you miss most?" asked my wife, trying to restart the conversation. He turned to her and said with his wet, old man's lips: "We believed that we were building a new society, that we were creating a safe haven for the Jewish people." Which meant, I miss the days when my most intimate words were the Zionist slogans; which meant, we were pioneers because of Zionism and Socialism, and because it was impossible to stay in Bessarabia on account of persecution by the authorities, the police and the local gangs; which meant, it's so hard to be old, all the more so to be old and surrounded by old age, illness, and death, which did not even exist in our vocabulary in those days. An old pride flashed momentarily in his voice, tinged with doubt whether my wife had heard from me about his glorious days as an emissary and a pioneer. Then both pride and doubt vanished in his usual plaintive tone, colored with resignation and helplessness. "It's incredible, what people are capable of when they're inspired with enthusiasm," he added in his own words, and again sank into his old man's silence. That enthusiasm had led him to believe that he was in the social vanguard, when in fact he was a small component in a doomed experiment. He imagined that he was the storm, when in fact he was a leaf that it blew away. Rest in peace, you hard, selfish, and naive man. I came to the funeral because it was important to Mom. I came to bury, not to mourn you. Don't make it hard on me now.

The Wheel Turns

"Yonah, rest his soul, came to fetch us from the hospital with a cart pulled by two mules. The cart sank near Ekron. The rain was coming down in torrents and you know there wasn't a road there yet. When we passed Ekron some women peeped out of windows and invited us to come in and spend the night, but I didn't want to. I wanted to get home. So I walked with him in my arms, wrapped in a raincoat that my husband, rest his soul, brought with him. Imagine, walking for hours in the rain and the mud, just eight days after the birth, straight from the *brith*. For weeks afterwards my legs were covered with bruises from the slapping of their raincoat. Well then, we finally got here in the evening. I put him in the baby house and went with my husband, rest his soul, to our room. That's what all the mothers did. In the morning I found his face covered with blood from the cold sores in his mouth."

Mom had told this story dozens of times, in early days with the pride of a pioneer who had overcome the forces of nature, later with astonishment at her own courage, and in recent years with anger. "And the poor man has had a cold ever since," my wife said, to hide her shock. But then she blurted, "This picture will haunt me all night." "So I won't be alone with it," Mom replied in a tired, disillusioned tone.

Tuesday afternoon. The house is emptying fast. Dinah and Elan said good-bye this morning, promising to return tomorrow. My wife and I were about to go home and from there to the airport. With Dinah gone, Mom felt like a hostess again and put on a white apron, as she used to do in the days when she was a children's nurse. "Can I ask you for something before you leave?" she said, and I encouraged her with a smile, as one does to a child. She took my arm and asked me not to disconnect our answer phone when my wife joined me in the States, so that she could call our house from time to time and hear my recorded voice. She grinned in embarrassment, as if she'd said something foolish, and did not notice that the smile on my face froze. When I was a small child we had a game: before putting me to bed in the children's house Mom would tie two shoelaces together and twine them between her fingers into marvelous shapes, tapestries, and hammocks, which she taught me to transfer to my fingers. Then she would tuck the brown laces into my pocket, so I would remember her till we met again the following evening. The laces were superfluous, because only a wall separated the children's house where she worked and the one I was in, and all day long I was surrounded by her absence. "It's a bit of a problem," I said. "People will leave messages and will be hurt when we don't call back. But I'll write you and phone from time to time. It'll be all right." Again I smiled at her, like an adult at a child. "There are only five weeks left to the summer vacation." She looked up at me, red-eyed, smiling.

"Have something to drink before you leave," Mom said, going to her little kitchenette. Raheli had not yet got over Mom's story about my reception at the kibbutz upon arrival from the hospital. I was familiar with the family mythology and only felt sorry for Mom and her naïveté. Did she realize that she had to leave her newborn baby in the children's house so as to demonstrate her unfailing devotion to the communal society? Did she know that in the eyes of the movement's leaders she and her comrades were the "desert generation," who must not be allowed to imprint their defects upon their children?

"I made this for you," Mom said, bringing slices of honey cake to the table. As a child I loved to taste the sweet coarse texture of the honey cake together with the chill smoothness of margarine, and now Mom put the margarine on the table and stroked my arm without a word. Seeing her reddish, round hand I was again struck by how she had shrunk in the past few years. With these fingers she would not be able to produce such marvels from brown shoelaces as she did half a century ago. Her childish fingers gave me the shivers. Suddenly the air in the room became familiar— the air that had been breathed and exhaled in tears and helpless rage, yelled out of contorted lips at a rejecting wall or fence. "Do you remember the shoelace you used to leave with me?" I asked. "Faigele mine, you still remember it? You were so small then!" A warm smile passed between us, the smile of old friends recollecting distant events in which they alone took part. Her side of it was asking if I understood that they believed they were building the homeland, and said, Look at my eyes—don't you know it keeps me awake at night? And my side was saying that when I visited my first children's house I understood that only the one who kicked you can take the kick away. It also said, Enough, it's all right, this account is closed.

An Israeli Sorrow

"Why are you slowing down?" my wife asked. We were approaching the Bnai Dror junction on our way to Evven Yehuda. The truck ahead of us was loaded with citrus trees. Sawed trunks, their bark grazed like the knees of a child who fell on the hard summer ground, slid back and forth with the vehicle's motions. A few leaves, like bits of paper remaining on an old notice board, fluttered in the wind. The bones of the branches showed white through the gray, lichen-crusted bark.

In the nearby village of Kfar Hayim my mother's hometown friend, Aharon Shpilberg, used to rise early in the morning, put on his heavy work boots, silently wind dusty khaki puttees around his ankles, and go out to the orange grove. At lunchtime he would take from the fridge a rectangular bottle of cold water and solemnly drink, gathering up the drops that fell on the table as if they were bread crumbs. In the evening he would come back from the field, his cart laden with corncobs for the small herd of cows he kept in the cowshed near his house, his face expressing the gravity of a man who knew he was doing the right, the destined thing. Across the way was the bus stop, shaded by two bitter-smelling cypresses, and there Elan and I would alight when we arrived for the summer holiday. A few steps away stood the stained structure of the village dairy. In the evening the villagers would drive over in their mule carts and bring in cans of milk, stop a while to chat, and quietly boast about their cows' yield or some innovation they had made in their hen coops. Further down the sandy road was a grocery, and beside it the village assembly hall. A notice board beside the administrative office announced in round handwriting a forthcoming movie, or a visit by an agricultural instructor. Once a week there was a movie, and once a week a lecture or a concert. Throughout the week the assembly hall wore an air of innocent, countrified pride. Known as "The People's House," its name preserved a solemn, festive echo that suggested a hidden relationship, like that of a secret order, connecting the people who gathered to see a movie or hear a lecture within its high, whitewashed walls. ("I'm going to a meeting in The People's House," Aliza, Aharon's wife, would announce, and a moment's silence would fall, as though the title made for a bigger space around the supper table than other words that had been uttered.) All around were bungalows surrounded by columned porches. A wooden door, closed with an iron hook, led from the porch into the house. Blackflies found their way in and hovered slowly in the cool interior. The neighbors' son, Yair, would help me collect the eggs in the Shpilbergs' hen coop, and I helped him in his parents' farm. Together we discovered the forbidden pleasures of smoking and a comradeship fostered by the mysterious, unattainable charms of girls. Every day a huge gray cat left the remains of chickens under the lantana bushes between the courtyards. One evening we managed to corner it in the cowshed and smashed its skull with a pickax.

What has happened to the Shpilbergs' corn field? When was the orange grove uprooted? "The People's House" has been turned into a shopping mall, that's all there is to it, I thought, and felt the past week's bereavement assault me from an unexpected angle. The Valley of Hepher has become a sprawl of plots for sale, a mass of shopping malls and branches of rival chain stores outdoing one another with their road signs. The facade of the shopping mall, overlooking the highway, was prettified with olive and orange trees, with old trunks and new branches. The fruit trees of my childhood have become ornaments, like African statuary or old plows from the Golan Heights that decorate villa gardens in Ramat Hasharon. Is my sorrow for the uprooted groves an Israeli emotion? Is it a romantic, Schiller-like melancholy? My wife laid her hand on my knee in sympathy. Reaching the Bnai Dror junction we turned left, toward Evven Yehuda. The citrus trees proceeded northward, further away, to the expanses of the built-up country.

Love

Dozing in the plane on the way back to the United States, I recalled Mom's request and said to myself that she was making progress, was trying to use modern communications. In the early nineties, when I had separated from my first wife and was living temporarily in a rented room in Tel Aviv, Mom was still leery of the answer phone. In those days the literary supplements still published poems:

Love

"Avremalé mein kind, we haven't
heard from you all week.
Faigaleh, are you eating all right,
all by yourself in Tel Aviv?"
She keeps pouring out her heart
into my answer phone.
My mother, her beauty lies
not in her seventy-five years
but in her love.
In the forties and fifties
she traipsed all over the land
for greetings
from remaining relatives
in Russia.
Then she became a skilful
writer and mainly reader
of letters:

upon their arrival
at kibbutz lunchtime,
then nightly, till
the next letter came.

The phone
she has never cared for—
an evanescent spirit,
unlike the solid written page.
Now with "Faigale mein"
she tries to soften
the machine's heart,
then falls silent.
I can see her hands
spreading open,
then dropping,
and my heart goes out to her.

A Miss

A Possible Journey to Bendery

A.

The name Bendery appeared on the lighted sign in three languages. My first impression on getting off the train is that this is no old-time "shtetl," but a substantial town. An East European town, to be sure, preserved pretty well as it was fifty and sixty years ago. The stone houses gleam in the sunlight, grayish-white like cotton trousers that have been washed and ironed too many times. The train station, with its pedimented roof and three big arched windows, is packed with people, and flanked by massive, flat-roofed stone buildings, abuzz with offices, shops, and stalls. The journey has left me tired. What am I doing here, in this strange town where my father was born in 1911. I walk down the dusty platform that I'd never expected to see. This is not the strangeness of emerging from a railroad station in a foreign country, of a foreign language spoken by inscrutable faces, but the strangeness between him and me. And yet, despite the distance, I feel intensely curious. For years I drove past the Bessarabian Jewish Community building in north Tel Aviv on my way home, and never once thought of stopping and looking in. Now I'm full of hungry curiosity.

B.

Bendery's market starts, as the book in my hand says, close to the station. All the produce of the fields around the town flows to this place, and now, in midsummer, the market overflows with watermelons (the elongated kind, like the ones we used to grow in the kibbutz many years ago), green and translucent-rosy grapes, and tomatoes so heavy they drop of their own weight. Some of the stalls offer the produce in plain wooden crates or fancy punnets, but it's the merchants whose produce lies in heaps on the ground who create the sense of abundance: piles upon piles of green, yellow, and stripey watermelons, and on beds of straw—stacks of melons and pumpkins which dye the winding market the color of honey. I withdraw from the commotion and stop a passing taxi, which takes me to the old Turkish fort, built in the north of the town in the fifteenth century and now stands desolate. Standing on top of the hill beside the fort I can see Bessarabia's fat fields, the light mist that floats over the deep green of the apple and pear orchards that stretch to the horizon. "This land is enfolded in a dark, sunburnt plain, quilted with dark brown furrows and well-watered. Blessed rains and abundant dew keep her pregnant. For most of the year she is heavily laden, yielding wheat and vine, fruit and vegetables, her cattle and sheep likewise fruitful."

I returned to find the market quiet: it's taking its siesta. A Jew carrying a talith under his arm directs me in Yiddish to Rabbi Itzikl's synagogue. Can the dark, polished stone of its facade be Jerusalem stone? The two miniature towers at either end and the cornice between them hint at the walls of Jerusalem near the Tower of David, as depicted on the embroidered silk cloths that cover the Sabbath hallah loaves. An explanatory leaflet informs me that such cloths are regularly sent here by the yeshivas in the Holy City. Inside, the western wall represents the Wailing, or Western, Wall, complete with the ashlars and the plants that sprout between them. A painstaking Odessan painter introduced the Jerusalem *kotel* to Bendery's market. And where is the courtyard of the great Rabbi Moishele Landman, the rabbi of the artisans and common people? I learned from an article that my father wrote in his memory that my grandfather, who was one of this rabbi's followers, had built this house and the synagogue beside it with money he raised for the purpose by selling lottery tickets. He was a fishmonger, and there was never a shortage of fish on the rabbi's table at the three Sabbath meals. I examine the blurry map, but it is of little use this time.

My impression that this is no shtetl but a proper town is strengthened by a walk through Bendery's high street, Kharozinskaya Street. Two- and three-story stone buildings line the wide road, with elaborate cornices under their pitched roofs, and tall lime trees shading them from the midday sun. I turn right on Konstantinovskaya Street towards the boulevard, the town's entertainment center. In the evening there will be a concert given by the local military band, with gypsy singers, and prosperous Jews and Christians will play cards in the local club. In the twenties and thirties young Jewish men came here in groups—a solitary Jewish lad was easy prey for the gentiles.

I close my eyes and try to imagine myself in this town in those days. It's a vain effort. To see this town through the eyes of a Jew who was born here, experienced persecution by the authorities and attacks by gentile hoodlums, and dreamed of faraway Eretz Israel, I'd have to be someone else, a totally different person. When I was a child I had a recurrent dream: a war broke out between Israel and its neighbors and Israel lost. I'd wake with a feeling of acute distress that lasted for hours. The War of Independence took place when I was four, but it seems that the sounds of that war and the words of the songs we sang made me totally identify Israeliness with independence. So now I find that I can walk about the streets of Bendery as an Israeli tourist, but cannot imagine myself in my father's shoes, as a Jewish lad coming to the boulevard and the auditorium in a group, and having to slink away after dark for fear of both policemen and bullies.

C.

The captain's calm, smug voice announces that we're approaching Orlando, and the flight attendant tells the passengers to straighten their seat backs and fold the trays in front of them. I shut the memorial book of Bendery and slip it into my bag. I feel a thin glass bursting in my chest. Why did I have to visit Bendery for the first time after my father's death? He had tried with all his might to become a non-Bessarabian, a kibbutz member. The effort drained him and left us no chance. We were like two strangers sitting opposite each other on a train, each one absorbed in a newspaper or sandwich, trying to take an interest in the fleeting landscape, with a casual glance at the other's book to discover if it is in one's own language, one's own nationality. In another place, at another time, we might have been able to exchange a few words, handshakes, addresses, perhaps family snaps.

Dry Sobs

When I said good-bye to my wife at the airport I knew I'd made a mistake: I should have found some opportunity to grieve, and didn't. The crowding in the children's home had taught me that showing one's feelings led to insults and mockery. Ten days before, when my wife told me that my father had died, I felt a dozen cold hands clasping my chest from inside. "I won't miss him," I said to myself, like a man feeling his limbs after a fall. The last days' pressure (hasty flight arrangements, finding someone to run the department in my absence, not knowing exactly when I was leaving and when coming back) began to ease, and utterly exhausted, I relaxed in the happiness of seeing my wife again.

When I entered the house Mom met me with the same embarrassed smile that had appeared on my face an hour earlier, when my wife told me about my father's passing. Dinah, herself a product of children's houses, was washing dishes, and turned around to smile at me—"The long-lost brother is here." Elan was sitting on the sofa, deep in conversation with an old classmate. He saw me from the corner of his eye, but went on talking. The summer before the mother of Yehoshua, an old classmate of mine, had died. Having just arrived for the summer vacation, I had missed the communication through the class network, and Mom told me about it the day after the funeral. I rang Yehoshua and told him that I'd only just heard, and expressed my sympathy. At that moment the difference between "I'm sorry" and "Please accept my condolence" was like the difference between two languages, between phrases that were possible or impossible between us. We fell silent for a moment. "Yes," he said in a thoughtful voice, and then went on, "And how are things with you? How is it in the United States?" and we both breathed more easily. Now, too, when I sat down at the table, Dinah and Elan asked me about the flight and the United States and my new job, and we looked at each other with relief at having successfully got through the renewed relationship with ourselves as orphans, feeling that we had reached a stable plane on which we would be able to walk securely throughout the shivah.

The next day I stood beside Mom and watched them lowering my father into his grave. There was an insulating layer around my chest, and nothing could get in or out. After the funeral I walked back to Mom's house, through the fields whose furrows and folds were the furrows and folds of my brain. On the way, in front of the vineyard which was in bud, I thought about the tears that remained out of reach, and wondered if that was how a man feels whose manhood betrayed him—remote and cut off from the source of his strength.

In the following days Mom was surrounded by people coming to comfort and console her, and we, the younger generation, sat with our guests with a grown-up smile, a smile of "let's not make a big issue of it," and "nothing's wrong." We are good at gestures of friendship, and an outsider wouldn't guess that our selfhood feels stressful, as rigid as a mask. Mom's friends fell on her neck and wiped off a tear, while ours slapped our backs with dry eyes and a confident, reserved smile.

I returned to the United States with excess luggage. I realized that I'd made a mistake: I ought to have found an opportunity to cry, and to do so in a friendly, Hebrew-speaking environment. The plane landed in Orlando in the late afternoon. In my haste, I'd failed to secure an onward flight to Gainesville, which left me facing another two-hour journey. Standing in line before a car-hire agency, I heard the name Gainesville, and suggested to the people who were renting a car to go there that we share it. I was glad not to have to drive, and they were happy to share the car with someone who knew the way. Their son had begun to study at the university, and this was to be their first visit there.

We got into the green Toyota and the husband—the hair on his nape trimmed as carefully as a French taxi driver's mustache—adjusted the driver's seat, checked the lights, and expressed satisfaction with the hired vehicle. The wife, an ageless American woman with her made-up face and wavy blond hair, tried out my name under her snub nose, as if tasting an unfamiliar food. I explained the difference between the Hebrew and

American version of the name. "You're from Israel, then?" the husband digested the information. "I always wanted to see Nazareth and Jerusalem." "It's never too late," I said, contributing to the chitchat between the fleeting acquaintances. "Say, Abe, isn't it kind of dangerous out there nowadays?" I was worn out from my journey and a long layover in Amsterdam airport, and wanted to let the sights of the road pass over me as over a mirror. "Dangerous, yes, my father died there a week ago," I replied, knowing I was breaking the rules of the game but unable to stop myself. "Oh I am sorry," said the man, glancing up at the rearview mirror and eyeing me with suspicion. "My sympathy," the woman said, examining me with her cold blue eyes. "It's never easy," the husband added. "No, it's never easy," I concluded with a slight sigh, struggling to maintain the ordinary, matter-of-fact exchange. The dry sigh turned into a cough and the cough into an unexpected shiver that spread from my chest to my shoulders. For a moment my shoulders sobbed soundlessly. I felt exposed and helpless. I remembered Chekhov's story about the poor man who tries in vain to tell casual passersby about his son's death, and at the end of the day pours his heart out to his mare. The memory raised a fleeting inner smile that steadied me. The husband and wife exchanged reassuring looks: might be awkward, sharing the car with a weeper Israeli. I took out a pen and the ticket envelope from my shirt pocket, and with my eyes smarting from the dry air on the plane, wrote: I should have found some opportunity to cry, if not for the loss of a beloved father, at least for the loss of a father, and if not for being orphaned by the death of a father, then for being orphaned by the death of a nonfather. I should have found an opportunity, and didn't.

About the Author

Avraham Balaban was born in Israel, where he finished his Ph.D. in modern Hebrew literature at Tel Aviv University. He has written seven scholarly books on prominent twentieth-century Israeli authors (including Nathan Alterman, Amos Oz, and A. B. Yehoshua), as well as on current postmodernists trends in Hebrew fiction. He is a prolific critic (more than 250 of his book reviews have been published in leading literary supplements in Israel and the United States) and poet. For his second book of poems he received the Prime Minister Award (1982) for creativity, and then was invited to Harvard as a visiting scholar in 1983. He taught for five years at the University of Michigan in Ann Arbor. Since 1989, he has taught modern Hebrew literature at the University of Florida, and, from 1996 to 2002, he also chaired the Department of African and Asian Languages and Literatures.